TREASURES OF ... S

Author's note

All the characters and situations described in this book are real, but occasionally I have given different names wherever people would prefer to remain anonymous.

Copyright © Jane Grayshon

First published in Great Britain in 1996

The right of Jane Grayshon to be identified as the Author of the Work has been asserted by her in accordance with the Copyright, Designs and Patents Act 1988.

10 9 8 7 6 5 4 3 2 1

British Library Cataloguing in Publication Data
A record for this book is available from the British Library

ISBN 0 340 65624 7

Typeset by Hewer Text Composition Services, Edinburgh
Printed and bound in Great Britain by
Cox & Wyman, Reading, Berks.

Hodder and Stoughton Ltd
A Division of Hodder Headline PLC
338 Euston Road
London NW1 3BH

Treasures
of Darkness

Jane Grayshon

Hodder & Stoughton
LONDON SYDNEY AUCKLAND

Acknowledgments

Quotation below title of chapter 7 by Henri Nouwen cited in *God: What the Critics Say*, edited by Martin Wroe (Hodder & Stoughton 1992).

Quotation below title of chapter 8 by Aleksei Leonov cited in *The Home Planet* (Macdonald & Co Ltd 1988).

Quotation below title of chapter 9 by Calvin Miller cited in *God: What the Critics Say*, edited by Martin Wroe (Hodder & Stoughton 1992).

Quotation below title of chapter 10 by Brian Keenan, *An Evil Cradling* (Random House 1992).

All psalms by Jane Grayshon quoted in this book are from *Faith in Flames* (Hodder & Stoughton 1990).

The unpublished poem by Dave Bookless in chapter 11 is reproduced with permission.

Unless otherwise stated, all Scripture passages are from the New International Version.

'I will give you the treasures of darkness,
riches stored in secret places,
so that you may know that I am the Lord,
the God of Israel, who summons
you by name.'

Isaiah 45:3

Contents

1

Stumbling into a mineshaft

God has a funny way of treating His friends
– a missionary on hearing that his wife had cancer

It doesn't matter what devastates us: what we notice
is that we feel devastated.

As I write today, I am thinking of several friends
who are stumbling, tripped up along their way. One,
a mother with three young children, has suddenly
developed the symptoms of multiple sclerosis. She
cannot see properly, hear properly, walk properly,
or feel properly. Her mouth, face and arms are
numb. Because of her husband's job, the family
have only recently moved house, which has meant
their being uprooted from their network of friends
and the stable life they had built up. Within days
of the move, and before being able to make any
new friends, this mother was admitted to hospital
for weeks of tests and treatment. Now she is home,
but not well. They have been on holiday by the
sea, 'away from it all', though their time together
was strained and difficult. Far from getting away
from the pressures of life, they have been hurled

more deeply into facing the very pressures they had hoped to escape, facing each day the appallingness of having a mum who is suddenly unable to laugh and cuddle and run across the sand as usual. It is as if this friend has fallen down a mineshaft. She does not yet know how deep this shaft may be, for she is still falling. She is afraid she may suffocate. Some days she has felt it would perhaps be better for her if she did. The way up seems too long, too hard for her already-exhausted energy.

Another's pain is very different. I am thinking of a man who is aware of his pain but is unable to identify it. He lives the life of a fit man, but he is burdened by a handicap he does not understand. In short, he cannot seem to be himself. He has gifts he dare not use. He wants to live an independent life but feels rejected whenever he is given autonomy: thus, he cannot win. A great, volcanic anger about this erupts from within him at the most unpredictable moments, causing a dark cloud to hover over his life – and that of his family. Christians pray for him and 'encourage' him in their talk of the healing God can bring. But the healing this man needs is much deeper and the process of receiving it is much more daunting to him than their quick words suggest. Few will accompany him along the road to becoming his true self; the moment has not yet come for him to allow even one person to do so. God's freedom remains a concept he hopes for rather than an experience he trusts.

A third friend, a middle-aged man, has given up all that he had in life in order to serve as a missionary in Russia. He and his wife have lived a very simple life in a tiny shabby apartment, trusting the God who has sustained them always. But his daughter is schizophrenic and, because of that illness, her baby has been taken away to be fostered. Now his wife, back in Britain for two months in order to accompany a Russian lady visiting Scotland, has just been diagnosed with cancer: Yesterday he was telephoned in Russia, told the news, and recalled from his missionary post there. Last night I met him at Heathrow airport on his way home – for how long? he wondered aloud as he sank into our car, looking more bewildered and jet-lagged than the passengers from long-haul flights. And to watch what ill effects of radiotherapy and chemotherapy? He was facing, squarely, life's mortality.

When instructing His first missionaries, Jesus said, 'Take no bag nor purse with you.' This man has relinquished, willingly, his bag and his purse in order to obey God. Now he is being asked also to leave those whom he loves in this life. An hour or so after stepping off the plane he turned to my husband Matthew and said, 'God has a funny way of treating His friends.'

It takes courage to face, squarely, our hurts. When we are tripped up in life, we hope we will be able to pick ourselves up quickly, dust ourselves down and carry on with life as before. Mostly we succeed and we can stagger onwards. 'Keep your chin up!' we tell ourselves. 'Every cloud has a silver lining.'

But occasionally such self-talk does not work. In fact, we cannot always hold our heads high and step jauntily through our days. Sometimes we watch with horror as someone close to us is tripped up by suffering in a way which renders them unable to get straight back up. It's as if the way which had looked perfectly clear has suddenly dropped into a hidden trap. We wonder what is happening and when we look, we see that the ground itself has given way. It's as if there is an earthquake. Before our very eyes our loved ones are plummeting into a great, gaping chasm. We cannot hold them back; they are already falling, spinning, cascading away from us, to be welcomed in the loathsome arms of the darkness below. We can but look over the edge of the yawning abyss and watch, and wait, and weep for their return. Or sometimes we do not watch, but we ourselves are the ones falling.

Another friend, Tony Larcombe, wrote to us some years ago just after his wife Jen had been taken into intensive care. One of his sentences stood out for me and for Matthew; it seemed to sum up how suffering makes us feel. 'It's as if I'm at the bottom of a mineshaft,' he said.

Matthew and I both feel as if we can identify with that description. The bouts of suffering which I have gone through have caused us both, separately, to experience what seems like falling down a bottomless pit.

In a mine it is dark; impossible to see ahead or even to the side. I have not seen who, if anyone, has been at my side. Seeing no-one, I have felt abandoned: abandoned by friends and abandoned by God. But darkness can deceive and perhaps there were friends alongside whom I could not see. Part of the agony is trusting, hoping, but not knowing; never knowing. And similarly with God. The agony of faith is that it is faith, which can never know. Knowledge is not faith. Faith trusts and hopes in the God we are told is ever-present but whom we cannot see. Doubt is so much easier to grasp than faith.

Darkness is so bewildering. In the dark we lose our orientation and become confused. We may put out our hands to try to feel our way along, but we may feel nothing. Or what we feel may be so unfamiliar that we can neither recognise it nor identify it.

Facts which we have always taken as immovable are suddenly questioned because they are no longer visible. Friends are distanced from us, either geographically (because of hospital) or by the uniqueness of our experience. Faith, which may once have been quite straightforward and, we thought, irrefutable, is suddenly put in doubt.

Billie Whitelaw, talking with Dr Anthony Clare on BBC Radio 4's *In the Psychiatrist's Chair*, discussed the effect on her of acting the play, *Not I*, in the dark. She described that particular dramatic presentation as a form of torture for her. The darkness was created very thoroughly. Both the theatre and her own body were completely draped in black. She was dressed in black clothing, including a black covering placed over her head, with only her mouth showing through. She was alone on the stage, which was given no background light. The whole theatre was dark: even its exit lights were shielded.

Billie was totally disorientated. Even though she was seated on a chair, she felt convinced that she was falling over, spinning round, upside down, tumbling eternally through the empty darkness. She felt, she said, as if she were in space, cascading eternally with no sense of place, of gravity. And whereas a space walker would have had the security of a life-line to the space-rocket, she felt she had none. When the blackness was complete, she had no hope of orientating herself.

Billie physically could not continue on the stage until she asked for a small, single light to be placed at the back of the auditorium. She survived her performance by focusing on that one glimmer of light although, even then, the effects on her were severe. She became hysterical and needed neurological treatment which she has continued ever since.

The playwright, Samuel Beckett, heard that a large Paris theatre wanted to show his play. Over delicious cocktails he wooed Billie, asking her, begging her, to act the part 'one more time'. She had to refuse. She had come to love this man and she wanted to please him above all else, but even though he pleaded with her she was adamant that she could not re-enter that darkness. The ordeal was too great.

If a person who is merely performing a play in darkness becomes so disorientated, how much more will someone whose pathway through life itself is through darkness?

How much more can we understand the times when we feel like telling God, the playwright of our lives, that we cannot go on in darkness! Even those who want to please Him above all else, sometimes want to be able to refuse Him. Yet the difference is that, unlike Billie's acting, in our real lives we have no choice as to whether we endure our darkness or not. God does not invite us out for cocktails, to woo us and then ask us, pleading with us to go along with our life in the way He has choreographed it. The so-called 'invitation' from God seems to emerge when we reach the point where we cannot take one more step along our own pathway through pain. But we have to. There is no way out; no give-up-and-do-something-else option. Then our darkness seems, in Billie's words, like a form of torture. Faced with intolerable pain, we cannot say no to God just because we have had enough.

I have tried. Exasperated, I have inwardly railed at Him, as I described in my earlier book, *A Pathway through Pain*. Everything looked as if God didn't care a toss how bad things were. He didn't seem to realise how bad 'bad' was.

'I can't take any more!' I said. 'Do you not understand? Can't!' But still the pain continued.

Why does God say that we will not have to face more temptation than we can bear? Why did Jesus say, so simply (simplistically?), 'Ask, and you will receive', when we *do* ask for things which we do not always receive? If only He had added the word, '. . . sometimes'! If only we could say that His Word is not true!

But God has told us, through Jesus, that He is the Truth.

Does God think we can bear what we feel we cannot? What kind of God is He?

And yet . . . and yet. Somewhere, somehow, another dimension creeps in as elusively as dew arriving on the grass.

God does not leave us railing. Everything suggests that He does; every feeling is of being left alone in our vulnerability, trapped by our bewilderment, frustration, and confusion. The darkness can cause us to feel so enveloped that our disorientation seems as complete as Billie Whitelaw's. We can more readily believe that we are dropping out of control through emptiness than that we are held in the hand of a loving God.

It is not so. It is more as if we were miners. Not that we have volunteered to descend to a coalmine (who would?); instead we have been pushed over the edge; ambushed. And however we reached the depths, like any miner, we find ourselves crawling along tunnels, fumbling, groping for our way.

Life is grim down a mine and we shiver with the strangeness and fear. Here we could so easily suffocate or fall again – possibly to our death. To take any action at all other than simply gasp for breath feels like the heavy work of a miner at a coal face.

Work is arduous, and heavy and dirty. We sweat until we stink from every pore. We have to search, and keep searching, to find the coal. Then we have to cut it away with occasional dangerous explosions, which we hope are controlled. They don't feel controlled. They feel too precarious; the ground all around shakes too much. We have read of plenty of miners whose lives have been lost in an accident.

Thus the family of the one down a mineshaft can never sit serenely at home awaiting his return. They worry lest, this time, he may be the one who does not return. He may be the one trapped, or drowned, the victim of some accident. They worry not because they fantasise, but because they know. Mining is dangerous; miners are at risk.

There is nothing either glamorous or romantic about this work. Miners do not slave away thinking to themselves, 'Ah, this coal will be so beautiful as it glows in the grate of someone else's hearth!' They themselves are not warmed, as they work, by the glow of a lovely fire. Their slog is a far cry from the quiet contentment which the treasure they are mining will eventually yield.

And even then, the fruit of their hard slog is not usable. Not yet. The coal has to be sifted and sorted from the useless rubbish. It has to be humped on to trucks and hoisted to the surface. Until that moment, all the work goes on in darkness, underground, unseen.

And so with treasures of darkness. The slog of enduring suffering is a far cry from the quiet contentment which should eventually follow. But while we are fumbling and searching, while our nails are splitting and our faces distorted at the effort of hanging on in there; somehow, when it seems that there is no purpose, no treasure – that is when we can have hope. Among all the rubbish and exhaustion, there are treasures. This is God's promise to Isaiah (45:3), 'I will give you treasures of darkness'. And one of those treasures is the revelation that God, the Light of the world, is not only in the light. When we do not find Him in the rescue where we hoped for Him to be, He is in the very darkness itself. This was Moses' experience, described in Exodus (20:21), 'Moses approached the thick darkness where God was.'

These treasures of darkness are not glib, or glittery, or glamorous. They are unearthed, sometimes unrecognised, through sweat and tears amid thankless, grimy underground work.

I do not believe that we earn these treasures of darkness. Our suffering does not win us merit points which we can accumulate until, eventually, we deserve a reward. They are a gift. They come to us by God's grace.

Perhaps it takes for suffering to strip us of the pride which lets us imagine that we should be recompensed for life's blows. After a time – in my case, many years – we gradually realise that some of the scales have been lifted from our eyes, just enough for us to see that our so-called achievements in life are but a folly. Whatever we have, or have not – physically, emotionally, spiritually – we are entirely dependent upon God's grace.

Perhaps this dependence is one of the treasures which I've found in my darkness. It has been born gradually, when all that was precious to me had been stripped away. Probably I should add that it was born reluctantly, too. I remember how I loathed the humiliation of being as weak and vulnerable as I was after a severe spell of illness. I had begged God to rescue me from such a state. But in doing so I suppose I was offering it into His hands. What a measure of His grace that He accepts as a gift that which we despise! It was in the process of praying thus that I realised I was asking God to lead me away from what had, in fact, become holy ground. So I wrote one of my psalms:

My life is on fire

and I am trapped
as by choking fumes
in a tunnel
from which I cannot escape

Pain burns, like a furnace,
until life's very substance
seems to turn to ash

And my faith is in flames:

Is it not folly
to trust still in a loving God?

Is it not folly
to know disappointment

yet still, to hope
in a hope that will not be disappointed?

. . . Yet, years on
these flames have never consumed

You have ignited
the dying embers of my soul
fanning them into inextinguishable hope

You've shown me
the mystery
of Your miraculous

This place of flames
is holy ground

And I can but bend
to remove my shoes
and worship You
. . . Holy God

2

Struggling for a blessing

*He that wrestles with us
strengthens our nerves
and sharpens our skill.
Our antagonist is our helper.*
– Edmund Burke after the French Revolution, 1789

Matthew felt crushed by a leaden apprehension as he walked away from my hospital bedside. He had kissed me goodbye, not knowing what the following day might bring. Would he see me again? In what sort of state? Still trussed up with tubes and oxygen and drips and pumps, clinging to life on this earth?

He had been telephoned by the hospital earlier in the day, and asked to come to the surgeon's office. There he'd been told that I was to undergo an emergency operation. It was one in a long line of major abdominal operations. The risk involved was high: only a few months previously, when I had been in a similar state, we had been told that it would be too dangerous to open me up again. But this time, the former restraint had had to be cast aside. This was a last resort.

'You can't!' Matthew had said to the consultant in reply to the news, his voice sounding cold in his attempt to overcome the desperation he had felt.

The answer had been considered and rational. 'It would be too dangerous for us not to.'

'She may not survive!'

'She won't survive if we don't.'

Matthew was distraught. Would this operation be the final straw at the end of my weary battle against repeated peritonitis? Would my fighting spirit be overcome one day; and had that day now dawned?

He walked to the car park and reached automatically for the hand of our son Angus. He held it tight, his hand dwarfing the small, nine-year-old fingers thrust so trustingly into his palm. Tangible comfort was not given; it was exchanged.

'Let's not go straight home,' he winked as he pulled the car door shut. 'Let's go and do something completely different; fun. How about a meal in a restaurant and then we'll go to a museum?'

Angus was too thrilled at the rare treat of a meal out to register his total gloom at the prospect of a museum. Restaurants were where rich people went, or adults on very special occasions; seldom had he ever been included in such a grandiose occasion, and never before alone with Dad. He grabbed at the suggestion with awed enthusiasm, postponing the grim thought of trailing round a museum while being what we called 'educated'.

It was an hour or so later that they arrived at the Northern Tate, a recently opened gallery in a renovated warehouse of Liverpool's Albert Dock. Matthew had shed at least the immediacy of his preoccupation with the hospital, having been soothed by the soft music from the white piano in the restaurant's corner. Angus had enjoyed the uninterrupted, chatty time together over his bowl of French soup, intrigued that at a restaurant people were allowed not merely to dunk their bread, but the bowl had actually appeared with a thick cheesy slice floating on top. Now, father and son walked hand in hand once again towards the entrance.

It was as they stepped through the door of the glass-panelled entrance that Matthew was stopped in his tracks. In the foyer in front of them, imposing in its centrality and waiting to greet them, was a life-size sculpture. The work, by Epstein, was an interpretation of the Old Testament story of Jacob wrestling with an angel.

Matthew took one look at it and gasped in awe. 'Wow!' he breathed.

Angus, ever polite, agreed.

Matthew remained still, stupefied, as if becoming a part of the sculpture himself. Here was a model of a man who, according to the biblical story, wrestled with an angel representing God Himself. For Jacob, the fight had occurred at night when he was terrified of what the next day might bring. It might have brought death: his twin brother Esau had wanted to kill him for years, and with good reason since Jacob had stolen his birthright and his blessing. Alone, afraid, sleepless through the hours of darkness, Jacob had been unable to wait passively. He had thrashed out wildly at God.

It was the solid strength of the two bodies which was most striking. Though only Matthew's own height, everything else about the structure portrayed immeasurable strength. It was huge and heavy. Crafted from brown marble, it was dull in colour yet compelling in its draw. There was no artificial light; no spotlight to enhance the sculptor's work. It was as if its presence alone, its great, weighty existence, was sufficient to catch the eye and arrest the attention of any who should pass that way.

This struggle between man and God was not something which could be avoided. People could avert their eyes and ignore it, but none could bypass its presence if they wanted to go further.

'Wow!' Matthew repeated. He stared, transfixed, allowing his mind to follow the thoughts evoked by the stonework. There, before him, with an immediacy which almost affronted the visitor, was a man who had given way to his urge to fight with unfettered zeal, with God.

Jacob had fought as Matthew wanted to. He had not fought politely nor with restraint, wrapping his feelings in nice-sounding prayers. Jacob was a man who went for God like a professional wrestler. He had flung himself at the angel, hurling his weight and thrashing at him. Jacob had had the energy which accompanies taking the lid off unfathomed anger. He had kicked and fought, his muscles straining and taut. This fight had been real, and urgent, and desperate. He had been dreading what the morrow would bring. And now Matthew felt involved in it.

At that moment Jacob seemed to be fighting on Matthew's behalf. Matthew began to walk round the sculpture, looking more carefully at some of the details.

The angel's arms were thrust underneath Jacob's, his muscles bulging with the force of his grip. It was a wrestler's hold which looked impossible to break.

The hands holding Jacob were huge and competent. The angel had spread them across Jacob's back, almost protectively. Matthew was unsure whether they were lifting up, or subduing, Jacob. Strangely, he observed, they were uncarved and unexpressive, compared with Jacob's. It was as if Epstein had felt it sufficient for them simply to be there, allowing the angel's strength to be felt.

So closely was the angel holding Jacob to himself that the smaller man's head had been jerked backwards, such that his neck was strained into an arch and he was forced to look upwards; heavenwards. But he was not looking heavenwards in awe; not while he fought against it. The position suggested that Jacob had perhaps needed to gasp for breath: perhaps, in his struggle, he had reached the point of suffocation. In every way, he was completely at the mercy of the angel. And the angel's face, like his hands, was strangely smooth, devoid of lines yet with a serenity which was hard to define. It spoke, silently, of a stillness which contrasted strongly with desperate fatigue.

And Jacob, of course, had no wings, unlike his opponent who could have risen when he willed. Jacob had nothing at his back. Nothing, that is, except the hands of the angel which held him in the very place where he was vulnerable.

Matthew cast his eyes down to the feet, which were large, and disproportionately so, providing each fighter with an extraordinarily firm base. The legs were rounded and thick, although it was absolutely clear whose were the stronger. While the calf and thigh muscles of Jacob were well-developed and sturdy, the angel's had a might and a latent power which was more than human.

Indeed, this edge of advantage was apparent in more aspects than just the solidity of the wrestlers' legs. The angel was a few inches taller than Jacob, and his shoulders were broader; and now that

Matthew looked more closely, he could see that the angel's feet were more firmly planted than his opponent's. Jacob had been lifted a tiny amount, until he was on tiptoe reaching upwards, and he was, therefore, slightly less stable. He could have been flung down at any moment.

But he was not flung down. Instead he was being held, and held closely. The two were locked in battle; there was a fight, yes, but there was such engagement between the two that they were fused. The marble was in fact one piece, not two. The whole sculpture could almost have been an embrace. Within the duel there was passion.

Had Jacob known that he was touching God? That he was being touched by God? Or was he so busy attacking, hitting out, expressing his inner turmoil, that he did not know Whom he was punching? Was he so consumed with anger and fighting spirit and fear of what the morrow would bring that he did not know the sacredness of the moment?

Matthew finished circling the work and stepped back once more. He was deeply impressed that this symbol should be given the entire space of the gallery's entrance. Because it stood on its own, centrally placed, it completely dominated the otherwise empty atrium. It was as if this fight with God had been credited with the significant place that it deserved. Nothing else was important in the presence of this. Everything else had been cleared away. It mirrored exactly the prominence of the struggle within Matthew.

After some several minutes Matthew took out his camera and began to take photographs of the statue. He took close-ups and wide-angled shots. He used almost an entire film. Indeed, after they had been developed, he had four of those photographs enlarged and he hung them in one corner of his study, the place where he kneels to pray each day. It is from the hours I have spent gazing on these that I have been given a glimpse into Matthew's thoughts at the time, for he has not felt able to articulate them. The images, he says, have represented the unspoken depths of his emotions.

What was happening in Matthew that he should be so grabbed by a piece of marble? What was it within him that was responding and resonating so deeply? Whatever it was, he was not ready to explore it immediately. It was many years before he could do more than look, and remember the feelings which he did not want to articulate. At the time, it was sufficient for him simply to repeat, 'Wow!', and take Angus's hand to walk round it and be absorbed into the scene.

This was one clue. Angus's presence was important. It reminded Matthew that he was a father. Many was the time he had been called upon to exercise his paternal strength in a scrap on the floor at home; to let his son experiment with exerting his strength, to let Angus feel big and important and manly, even as a toddler, and to sense also the security of the greater, more dependable, strength of a father.

At the gallery while holding Angus's hand Matthew was potently aware of being the one being depended upon. He had the role of the fatherly one who could take whatever displays of emotional strength came rushing out of his child, however wild or ugly they may be. He was the one to soothe, to nurture, and to understand. He was the one to know that it would be because of love that a child would feel secure enough to show his father how deeply hurts can run; how strongly energy can pulse through a boy's veins. He was the one to demonstrate the greater strength: strength which chose to be gentle, which knew how to withhold the mortal injury he could deliver.

As the scales fell from his eyes Matthew recognised that whatever was true of an earthly father was also true of his heavenly Father. He recognised that this was how God loved him with gentle strength. His Father waited to engage with him. That day, it was as if God took Matthew by the hand and whispered, 'Have a look at this, son. You're ready to understand a more grown-up stance now.'

Jacob had needed to fight with God. He had needed to vent his pent-up emotions; in the darkness of his circumstances he had needed to wrestle, and to hit out at God in that inner turmoil. He gave God all that he had. He lashed out at God, writhing and kicking with all his strength. No doubt it was not just his strength, but with all his heart, mind, and soul, too. As he had done so he had given himself, consciously or unconsciously, into the hands of God. Had others been watching they may have disapproved of such an ugly scene. 'You can't offer *that* raw emotion to God! Especially not anger towards *Him* – that's no "gift"!'

Jacob gave himself into God's hands just as he was. And God accepted him just as he was. He accepted Jacob's need to fight, and He rose to it, locking Himself in the battle and encircling him in His arms. He led Jacob to keep giving right up to his limits. That was the beginning of Jacob's transformation.

Jacob may have thought he was fighting against God; he discovered that in fact he was fighting for Him. Through the darkness of the night, he acknowledged his need for God like a growing thirst. By the end of the struggle, he would not let the angel go until he had been blessed. This was when the dawn began to break. In his darkness, the urgency of his need *for* God became as desperate as his original urge to fight *against* Him. What began with hurt became the means of his healing. After he had admitted his need for God – and not merely admitted it, but begged for it! – he began a new era in his relationship with God. From this time onwards the descriptions of him indicate that he had the qualities of servanthood towards God, His own God, in place of activity for God, the God of his father, Isaac and his grandfather, Abraham.

My own discovery of this has been through a different route but, as Jacob, I have struggled and been afraid before finding a resting place. My frustration was at the enforced inactivity of profound illness which prevented me from fighting my way through life. I thought that seeking God had to be a fight; I thought that resting in prayer – even sleeping in prayer – was a measure of failure. I suspect that I despised the impotence I felt at being still and knowing that God was God. I wanted to *do* lots, and know Him! Gradually, very gradually, I am learning to allow myself to be held in my angry tantrums, until slowly, suspiciously, I am beginning also to depend on that gentle but inescapable hold. It is thanks to God's grace, rather than my truculent reaction, that my struggling is eventually giving birth to a new and unexpected contentment.

Hungrily
I seek You

to learn of You
to feed from You
greedily

And as I read
and as I write
    I am drawn close
    by Your arms
    held
    as a babe

who, having suckled,
drops into sweet slumber:
filled, for that hour,
in deep contentment
with naked embrace of intimacy

    Lord, may my seeking
    not be only frenzied activity;
    Teach me contentment
until I am not ashamed
to find myself slumbering
    in Your hold

The wounding God

Yesterday I was looking at Matthew's photographs of the Epstein sculpture. 'Why did you take this close-up of Jacob's hands?' I asked, pointing to one of the enlargements.

'Because they're just hanging there,' replied Matthew. He came over to study once again the way they dangled limply. 'They were tired,' he said, and he smiled with a glint of self-recognition. 'They've stopped fighting.'

Perhaps the climax for Matthew, as for Jacob,

was the moment of reaching the end of his own strength. To win was to sense his weakness and be held by One Who offers His strength.

There is something else which I see in the photographs which Matthew did not notice himself, and nor did I when the opportunity came for me to look at the statue for myself in its 'home' in the London Tate Gallery. In the corner of the angel's eye the marble is darkened – I assumed at first that it was a blemish – but the line of darkness has the shape of a tear on the point of falling down the angel's cheek.

Increasingly I suspect that that tear is no blemish; no accident. Deeply engrained in the very fabric of the angel is an expression of sadness over a love that Jacob could not sense and did not want to receive.

Jacob was unaware of the longing in the angel's eyes. So busy was he fighting that he could not see the gentle tenderness with which God encountered him, drew him, welcomed him, held him and embraced him – all on Jacob's terms.

Jacob was unaware that wrestling with God necessarily included being touched by God. He imagined that, to emerge from the struggle and face the new day he feared, he needed something else – a blessing – to take with him to hold on to, perhaps as proof that something had happened during the hours of darkness. So busy was he demanding the touch of blessing he did not acknowledge that he was being touched already; and not merely on that night, but ever since he was a boy and had stolen a blessing via the hand of his dying father.

Jacob was unaware that engagement with God was the stuff of life. As the dawn approached he became agitated, saying, 'Must dash! I've got a job to do. But first, bless me . . . !' He was unaware that meeting His Maker was the source of his daily work, and that he could never step out of the presence of God no matter where he went.

Jacob was unaware that God had restrained Himself. God had not flung him down as he could have. He had protected him and strengthened him by His hands holding him. Jacob had been so busy trying, vainly, to get the upper hand on the angel, he could not see how he was being blessed.

And Jacob, in his naïvety, did not see any of that. In his night of fear, he presumed upon God and demanded a blessing as if he were God. He became impertinent; maybe he always had been. He had cheated his brother and his father since boyhood, and cheated his uncle in his business deals, always grabbing at what was not his. That night he tried to grab from God what was not his, and he put the sovereignty of God on the line. He got more than he bargained for. He was blessed, yes; but the evidence of the blessing was the burden of a limp.

Blessed by a limp

God asserted His sovereignty, giving one touch on Jacob's hip which gave just a glimpse of what He was able to do. With that one touch He stopped Jacob in his tracks. Always before Jacob had run away: from Esau, from his uncle Laban, from God Himself. Once his hip was dislocated, he could no longer run.

Jacob begged for a blessing; he got one, but not the kind he wanted. He was forgetting that he had already been blessed, and been promised more: blessings pressed down and running over. He had lived all his life as if God were relevant only to his father, Isaac, and his grandfather, Abraham, rather than to himself. He could not bring himself to put the weight of his own trust in God, preferring always to trust his own skill.

After Jacob's first dream of the ladder to heaven God had spoken to him very clearly, promising, 'I am with you and will watch over you wherever you go' (Genesis 28:15). Jacob behaved as if he were on his own, and as if God were not with him. He had made money in devious ways, as if God were not watching over him.

God had said, 'I will bring you back to this land.' Jacob had returned to it as if he were running away from his mistakes, not as if God were drawing him, leading him, bringing him.

God had said He would do what He was promising. Jacob had lived as if God might not; or at least, as if he had to deceive, cheat, manipulate in order to ensure that these things would happen. He lived as if God were not strong enough to do His will without Jacob's help.

In their fight, God made himself known despite Jacob's lack of faith. He showed that He was not merely strong enough, but stronger.

Throughout the fight, Jacob had wanted to show his strength; when he demanded a blessing he surely did not want to look weaker as a consequence of it. But the blessing was a limp. Jacob was given a reminder that God's strength is made perfect in our weakness.

So Jacob received what he did not want; what he had resisted for the whole of his life. He felt his place before God. It was a blessed place to be. But we do not always appreciate the holiness of the ground on which we are standing.

Matthew talks of his frustration of knowing that God could not be defeated, yet also, paradoxically, the security because He couldn't be. On that day in the Northern Tate, the awfulness for Matthew was that he knew that he could not command God to save my life. He knew that he was no longer able to claim things in prayer, as if he were in charge and God had to obey him. Matthew had glimpsed God's holiness, and he knew that God was sovereign. Epstein's statue was quite clear: God's superiority is constantly, if silently, asserted. He is always the greater. He is in control.

To stumble across the sovereignty of God, however unwillingly, is a treasure in darkness. I often wonder if Jacob knew the blessing of his limp, or whether the burden of it blinded him.

> I pray for Your strength
> And You give me weakness
> Telling me that that is how
> Your strength is made perfect
>
> I pray for Your riches
> And You give me poverty
> Telling me that that is how
> Your kingdom is found
> I pray for Your life
> And You bring me to the brink
> Telling me that Your Resurrection
> Was born out of death
>
> > My Lord and my God
> > Your ways are not my ways
> > I can but respond
> > With thanks from my heart.

3

The hours of darkness

I was angry in case God thought
this was good for me
– a mother whose baby had died

There is a phrase which Scots love and which I, having been born with Scottish blood in my veins, heard frequently in my early life: 'The man who pays the piper calls the tune.'

I quote the phrase now because I sometimes feel that we get confused as to who deserves to call the tune in the symphony of our lives. Is it God, or is it ourselves?

Sometimes I have the impression that Christians think of God as the piper who plays for our benefit. Like any piper He turns our walking into dancing, bringing a spring to our step and a joy to our life. We consider that we 'pay' Him by our prayers and our worship. While things go well we can exult in our relationship of mutual giving to one another. If things go badly we consider we have the right to tell God, we don't want that tune; we don't like it. Thus our prayers include requests for what we would like Him to change.

Sometimes it seems as if God puts His holy foot down, digs in His heels, and does what He decides no matter how much we order Him otherwise. There is a clash of wills. Such a time is, I think, one of the biggest traumas we ever face in our spiritual lives.

I confess that it was a relief to me when I first realised that I was not the only person to face this turning upside-down of my previous faith. A very close friend, Sarah, went through a similar disorientation, and then reorientation, with God. I shall never forget the agony of being the bystander, watching her battle alone; and nor shall I ever forget how the pain of watching gave way to awe and wonder.

'But *how*, Jane?' I remember her asking me one evening as we chatted beside a log fire on a wintry evening. We both welcomed our probing conversations. 'How *can* we have courage when God seems to ask intolerably painful things of us?'

How could I answer her? I feared giving insensitive 'answers' to what was painful indeed. Sarah had every reason to talk about needing courage. All evening my eye had kept being drawn to the enormous brown cord sag bag, poignantly vacant in the corner by the window. It was the one she had used to lay each of her babies in their early months, after they had drifted off to sleep in her arms.

On the solid wooden sideboard at the far end of the room stood the photographs of her husband and family. The children were a prominent part of their lives. But the beaming infant framed by the most elegant silver frame made my heart lurch with the weight of grief. Robert's bubbling little life had been snuffed out.

It had been in the March, two years previously, when Robert had become ill. He was eleven weeks old when, suddenly, his life had been threatened by a bleeding disorder. Everything had happened so quickly. From an ordinary visit to the family doctor one day, Sarah had found herself with her longed-for baby, hurtling by ambulance down the street towards hospital. She had felt utterly bemused and disorientated. For hours which had smudged into bleary days she had been mesmerised, engulfed by fear at all the activity going on around her son's cot. However, sophisticated as the medical treatment had been, it had been to no avail. Before her horrified eyes, Robert's life had ebbed away. Within two days he had died.

The following day had been a Sunday. Mothering Sunday.

Colin and Sarah had felt wounded and hollow. They had stayed away from church; they had been unable to face anyone who might have told them to be thankful for the children who remained. That would have seemed like denying their grief. The burial had been simple, and only snowdrops marked his little grave.

How could I answer Sarah's questioning two years later, without trampling on her feelings like a bull in a china shop? Except that she wanted – needed – to wrestle with her bewilderment.

I turned her query back to herself. 'How did you manage to have courage at the time?'

Sarah shook her head. 'I found it so hard.' Her eyes were heavy with sorrow recalled, and she spoke her words hesitantly, in spurts. 'God seemed to be asking too much of me,' she stammered. She pursed her lips together and sighed, not with resignation but with exasperation at how God had treated her.

'He seemed to want intolerably painful things for me.' She glanced up quickly to check my face, afraid lest she had shocked me, but she must have sensed from my stillness how closely I could identify with her. Honesty before God has always been vital to my own journey. After all, He is able to take our fighting against Him, and hold us, and not fling us down. How can we reject our friends while they are saying strong things against God, when He doesn't?

'I was afraid that God might dismiss my feelings,' Sarah went on, her voice trembling like that of a rejected child. Her eyes were fixed on her chair. 'Dismiss them as if they didn't matter, or as if they didn't count so much as His. And I was supposed to trust Him! It made me feel desperately alone.'

There was a long silence. The flames in the fireplace licked around the chunks of wood like tongues. One log slipped down with a raw, scraping noise, and nestled more closely into the grate.

I could share Sarah's sense of abandonment by God. When He has not given the pain-free solutions for which I, and my situation, have begged, my dismay has been profound. It seems that He pursues what He thinks is best, and we have to yield to His way. All is supposed to be well if we trust Him. What hurts is that it also seems, sometimes, as if He doesn't mind how much His way hurts us.

It takes me back to my nursing days. Some of the more callous nurses didn't seem to mind when they had to administer injections which were painful (intra-muscular vitamins were renowned for being painful!). The temporary soreness was so trivial to them, they didn't really address the issue with their patients. They would tell patients just to be glad that the injection would make them better. There was no room for sympathy.

Sometimes it appears that God doesn't mind the sore moments we feel, even if those moments stretch on for days, or months, or even years. He seems not to dwell on how bad our soreness feels, because His interest lies in the good He is doing. And we squirm, and squeal, because we are yelling at Him about what hurts, begging Him to take it away, knowing that He could if He wanted to . . . but He doesn't always. And usually, in such darkness, we do not see what on earth is the point. We do not even see what is the heavenly purpose. More often than not, we do not see any good at all, even in the end; or if we say we do, we have to stretch our imaginations.

People have come to me after I have spoken at meetings, saying, 'Oh, but Jane, just think of all the good that's come out of your illness! Think of your speaking, your writing, how it's helped others . . .' But I am human. I am not altruistic. If I have helped others, that does not make the years of pain worth while. The illness was too dreadful for that. At the time, our suffering seems to be a terrible waste, and absolutely futile. These were Sarah's words when I asked her gently how she had got through.

'It all seemed such a waste, so futile,' she replied, closing her eyes against the painful memory. 'I was angry at the idea of having to go through with watching Robert dying: angry in case God thought it was "good for me" or something.' Her voice trailed off. Time had not eradicated the fact that there had been a bitterness within her; she could not deny it as she recalled that fateful March.

'So why didn't you stop trusting Him?' I pursued.

She sighed, a heavy sigh which acknowledged the fact that she was still torn in her mind. Then she looked up. 'In among all my anger at God there was a question. It kept repeating itself with stark simplicity: "Do you believe in the goodness of God?"'

I was silent, intent as Sarah bared her soul. 'All of one night beside Robert's cot,' she said, 'I remember looking helplessly on, weeping and sobbing. I felt as if I'd reached rock bottom by then. I cried out, "Lord, please don't ask me to go through with Robert dying!" And there was no response; only the constant repetition of the question, "Do you believe in the goodness of God?"'

Sarah's eyes were brimming with tears once again. 'Somewhere – somewhere – among all my fear, I was aware of a flicker of hope. I knew it had to be a lie to imagine that God would impose dreadful things on me, disregarding me. It seemed as if He was, but deep down I knew it wasn't true. To acknowledge the lie was like the glimmering dawn light. I had to concede that His purposes are for good and not for evil.'

It was my turn to look down, avoiding the penetration of her gaze while I listened. I was inspired but also strongly challenged. How would I have responded if I had heard the same question as Sarah, with such a persistent demand for me to choose? I shuddered to think of having to bear a loss such as hers. Would I have found the same peace? I might have shared the doubts she'd expressed earlier, that God had taken her further than she felt able to endure; but her faith seemed so strong!

She had resisted the lure to believe that God was letting her down.

Did I believe in the goodness of God as Sarah did?

Sarah must have read my thoughts. 'Don't get me wrong – it was desperately hard,' she tried to explain.

I grunted an acknowledgment. I wanted to hear what had been the turning point for her.

'And then?'

'Jane, the only peaceful course for me was to trust in God's goodness.' She lifted her shoulders and almost laughed at herself, still unable to explain away the paradox with reasoning. She could hear for herself that her faith sounded as if it had been strong, but she also knew that at the time it had felt pushed to the point of doubt.

Do we believe in the goodness of God?

I have never had to go through what Sarah has, losing a child, yet I could identify with what she said about the starkness of God at such a time. Perhaps our inability to share one another's circumstances is not nearly so important as our ability to share the depths to which our situations take us.

Sarah's story was of her making an important choice, but it sounded nevertheless as if God had been somewhat ruthless over the cost to her.

How can a God of love allow this? We cannot say. If we knew the answer, we would be satisfied. We would never need to hit out at Him in words again. Our struggle with Him, or with His angels, would comprise an embrace without the anguish.

But the question remains, and it raises itself

at every tragedy. When I was first qualified in nursing, I worked as a Staff Nurse in a children's ward in Edinburgh. That hospital had a famous radiotherapy and chemotherapy department which was then the centre for the whole of Scotland, and visiting officials used to be shown round our ward to see what was done for the children with cancer. And they would stand at the doorway into the dormitories, and they would see the terrible sight of those children who were too sick to be out of bed. They would see the young faces, pale and listless, their hair falling out with the chemotherapy, their thin arms poking out of the bedclothes like sticks on the white sheets. And these visitors would shake their heads and mutter, 'How can a God of love allow this?' The question was rhetorical, for they weren't asking God, and nobody on this earth can speak for Him.

But one of the privileges of nursing was that we did not have to stand at the doorway, watching from a distance. We were allowed right up to those bedsides and, usually, we could do at least something to ease those children's lives, and their deaths. But more important than that, we could listen to what they said, and we could marvel at their wisdom. Seldom did those children – particularly those who were dying – feel sorry for themselves. They endured their present suffering and, with naïve and innocent delight, looked forward to their future, whether that was to get better on earth or get completely better in heaven.

I shall never forget one boy whose dying taught us all so much. As his life slipped away, his mother sat by his side, keeping vigil. She was what Scots call brave, keeping her tears in check. On his final day on earth, however, when she saw the unmistakable look in his tired eyes, she broke into weeping. The sister in the ward took her aside and told her she must try not to burden her son so, for he was only six. But the effect of that instruction did not last for very long; the mother was too distressed to blink back all her tears. It was her own son who helped her. I remember seeing him take her hand – it was not the other way round – and he was the one to reassure her. 'Don't worry, Mummy,' he whispered. 'Jesus is looking after me, you know.' Then he added, 'Don't you want Him to look after you, too?'

It would be easy to dismiss what he said, saying his faith was 'sweet' but that he just 'didn't know' about real life, or real suffering. However I believe that he knew what it was like more than many adults! Out of honour for him as he left his body, his mother began to think about what her little boy had said. She stopped shaking her head and tutting at God. She stopped demanding simplistic answers, for she knew nothing could fill the deep thud in the pit of her stomach. She dared to trust what he had said, and be challenged by what he had asked. Instead of letting her son be the only one to reach out his hand, she too began to offer her hand into what was, quite honestly, darkness. Mysteriously, miraculously, that bedside was transformed to a very special place; hallowed ground.

I cannot say what, exactly, that mother experienced in her soul. I was not close enough to share her inner journey. I was merely a nurse, watching. All I can describe is the evidence of peace which settled upon her, and the turnaround in her attitude from resenting her parting from her son, to sharing his joy at his home-coming to heaven itself.

Sarah, two years after Robert's death, was more able to articulate her turning-point. Everything in her had felt that she knew – better than God – that for her baby to die was not the best plan. Her plan was better: to save Robert's life. I do not know how, but for some reason God did allow that death. The deceit was for Sarah to believe that God didn't realise how grim that felt. The deceit was for her to believe that He didn't care, that His will was to call for a punitive life so Sarah's faith could be purified.

The truth which did in fact set Sarah free – free to be sad and to grieve, and free from resentment towards God – was that God is good. He does not explain why He allows hard things; but then, nor does He explain why He gives us His blessings, which arrive as unexpectedly and, apparently, as randomly as illness. God does not consider Himself to be answerable to us. But He does ask us to put our trust in His promises, not to satisfy our reason, but as a starting-point. He has promised each of us that His steadfast love will never come to an end. So if all else fails, if everything in our lives goes wrong and all evidence points to God seeming to be cruel, then the truth will still stand. It seems that that is the point at which He asks us, do we still believe that His purposes are for our good, and not evil?

We cannot answer that question until our faith is tested. It's one thing to believe in the goodness of God when the evidence all around is of answered prayer and blessings in abundance. It's quite another when prayers are left pending and blessings are not yet evident. It's the difference between 'I see, and therefore I believe' and 'I do not see, yet I believe.'

Jesus said to the no-longer-doubting Thomas,

'Blessed are those who have not seen and yet have believed' (John 20:29). Sadly, many Christians in our churches imply that such people are to be pitied; that they are in need of ministry. I am thinking particularly of those involved in the wave of the Holy Spirit which is associated with Toronto since 1994. After seeing manifestations of God's Holy Spirit, people become thrilled – and rightly so – because they have seen and felt the goodness of God. But being bowled over by God in this way is not the whole story. Their thrill can occlude another aspect of God's ways. They can regard those who are clearly touched by the Holy Spirit as having been blessed: the vocabulary of the whole 'Toronto blessing' underlines this. Those whose worship is only a response to seeing His goodness are slower to recognise the kind of blessedness which Jesus described.

Jesus said, 'Blessed are those who have not seen and yet have believed.' In our times of darkness, of not seeing the goodness of God, our belief is put to the test. Our faith is then blind faith; faith which is beyond reason. But blind does not mean naïve.

It's hard to put our weight on what we believe. I am reminded of a visit with our daughter Pippa to the London Science Museum where, in one room full of experimental science, we were presented with some soft plastic bricks. Each brick was shaped like a giant-sized chunk of tinned pineapple with one end narrower than the other. The challenge was to build a bridge across a five-foot gap between two walls. There were only five of these flimsy 'bricks', and at first the idea of success seemed absurd. However with a bit of thought we saw the skill: to place the pieces with the narrow edges together. With the wide edge uppermost, the bridge could not fall down.

Building the arch was one thing; we were then asked to walk across to test it! The bricks' material was so soft, I was convinced that a structure as simple as that would collapse under our weight.

We held our breath as Pippa crossed the arch first, clutching tightly to my hand, balancing a few feet above the safety of solid ground. Would it hold? It did! And then it was my turn to step out and cross it. Again – to my profound relief! – it held. Indeed, the more we walked, the more our weight pushed the wider edges down, pushing the bricks more tightly together so the whole arch was held more firmly.

It is rather precarious to put our weight on what we claim to be our faith. As the Science Museum experiment demonstrated, it seems preferable to stand back and admire the theory than to trust what we believe so much that we dare to put our weight on it. It is safer not to step out than to walk where we could fall badly.

On the arched bridge, I could not see what was happening to the bricks when I first walked gingerly across. My heart was in my mouth in case the whole thing collapsed. Only the observers, standing at the side, could see and could tell me it was not dangerous. They sounded as if they had no idea of how precarious it all felt to me! But because they could see what I could not, they were in a position to understand far more than I could without their perspective.

I wonder whether onlookers who watch our walk of faith see in us what we cannot see in ourselves. When we turn to God, we do not always see Him; when we stretch out our hands to Him, we do not always feel Him. But when we pray in our moments of desperation, running more deeply than our doubts, lies a hope at a level beneath our sense of desolation. We often do have a deep sense that God is there. Even though we may resent having to wait before we 'feel' any different, we know that hope will eventually dawn.

This has been my experience. In desperation I have begged Him, please, to heal me as He has healed others. I began by supposing that if He answered me, my hurt would be soothed away and my tears wiped away. It took a long time – maybe months, maybe years, I'm no longer sure – to be convinced that when He removes the terribleness of our suffering, He is with us in it no more than when He does not.

If I am honest I should admit that this seemed, at first, rather useless of God. It looked as if He was giving me a diluted version of blessings when He gave others full strength healing. What took time to discover was the consolation: that the light shines *in* the darkness. When we have lost sight of God altogether we fear Him to have withdrawn; in fact He has embedded Himself in the darkness within us where we fear even to look. The place from which we want to escape may be the very place where He is waiting to be found.

When God did not remove the desperation of my pain, and when that crescendoed so that it seemed to consume my conscious moments, that very desperation was all I could offer to God in prayer. It was all I had! But then, Jacob gave God all that he had – an ugly fight – and God accepted his offering as if it were a gift, and in holding him there He was transforming him.

So I, too, began to offer all that I had, pathetic as it may sound. One of my psalms was written in bed as I felt myself wince at every breath. Its importance to me was the recognition that, when we think we have nothing to offer to God, we can offer even that.

> Do not kiss me now
> Do not come too close
> It's every breath which I must breathe
> Now
> and again now . . .

> > I hear a groan with each one:
> > Is that my voice?
> > I do not mean to grunt.
> > If I hold my breath
> > Does that help?
> > . . . I cannot.
> > My body's past such pride.
> > Instead I'll delay each one . . .

> Just stroke me now:
> My arm
> My forehead
> Run your fingers through my hair.
> Without words,
> Soothe me
> Reach me
> in this world with no words
> this world where tears will not flow
> for anguish

> > Ah! Staccato stabbing
> > Pain piercing
> > Throbbing
> > Punctuated by these cries

Suppressed
But not silenced.

Would that this were singing
and not a cry of distress!
Oh my God; my God! . . .

Accept each groan
each involuntary groan
and make it into
a song for you.

Darkness does not feel like a treasure. In fact, I do not think it *is* a treasure. The treasure emerges when, through the darkness, we discover that even the blackest times cannot separate us from the love of God. His goodness is not wiped away by our feeling of loss. But perhaps at the time we may not recognise this as having any value; it may at first look exactly like the rubbish from which it still has to be sifted.

4

The dawn of hope

But hope has *disappointed me!*
And God has disappointed me!
– myself, facing a hysterectomy, aged twenty-four

I once went to a concert at the Royal Liverpool Philharmonic Hall to hear Tchaikovsky's fifth symphony. My knowledge of composers' lives is shamefully scanty, but the programme notes for this concert certainly caused me to stop and think.

Tchaikovsky was a homosexual and, apparently, one of the reasons for the despondency which can be heard echoing through his music was that he could not stop himself from promiscuity. He tried sincerely and repeatedly throughout his life. Hope would spring up each time he made a fresh decision to try again. When he felt he was succeeding in overcoming the temptation, he married, determined to live as he believed he should and as he hoped he could. But he failed: failed his wife, and failed himself. His hope proved empty.

According to the programme notes, this story of unfulfilled hope is reflected in Tchaikovsky's fifth symphony. The theme tune at the end is the same as at the beginning. The notes concluded in explanation, 'Tchaikovsky follows the line of hope to its end, only to find he has come full circle.'

Hope did not spring eternal for Tchaikovsky. There came a point when it had been disappointed once too often; it became exhausted. He became disillusioned, then, and he despaired. He expressed his private, inner tragedy in his most poignant, sixth symphony, which is commonly regarded as his own requiem. Within days of its first performance, he committed suicide.

I wrote at some length in *A Pathway through Pain* about my own experience of a consuming, devastating disappointment. Since that book was published, I have heard from many people whose hopes have been dashed, who describe feeling as wrecked and battered as flotsam strewn across rocks after a storm. They are the sorts of people whom we meet every day: people in pain, physically and psychologically; people tortured by grief, or loneliness, or their hatred of themselves. Some face death, some a living hell. The ones who are desperate feel dismissed by those who say, so simply, 'Cast your burdens on the Lord, for He cares for you.' I wonder how often I, too, may have hurt someone because I have uttered ill-timed words of wisdom too easily.

Does God expect us to keep hoping when we keep bumping into repeated disappointment? Is it naïve of Christians to say, 'Just hope in God'? Are they blind to what desperate disappointment means, if they can talk as if hope were easy?

For six months during 1980, between February and July, I was in hospital with acute peritonitis. The surgeons did as much as they could during an operation at the outset of that episode, but they had to sew me up leaving a mess of pus and inflammation all over my abdomen. When I did not respond fully to the aggressive antibiotic treatment, hope for my recovery waned. My life was balanced between life and death.

I felt very ill. I knew that to die would have been gain. I was so ill, there was little reason left for me to want to continue on this earth, especially when the prognosis was more pain, and more surgery, even if I should recover. All I hoped for was release, whether that meant release from this life into heaven, or relief from excruciating pain into a better life here on earth. I was desperate for one or the other.

Neither happened. I dragged on in hospital, uselessly, wasting my life, wasting my gifts. I saw no end. I was at a loss. What could I hope for?

I thought of Job, a man in the Old Testament who was noted for his close relationship with God and for the holiness of his life. Even a man as holy as he had reached the point of articulating the sort of hopelessness that I felt. 'My days . . . come to an end without hope' (Job 7:6). I pitied his having had to endure his non-understanding comforters telling him to 'Be secure, because there is hope' (Job 11:18). I had heard such advice myself; each time my 'advisers' had considered their counsel to be fresh and innovative. *Plus ça change, plus c'est la même chose*, I thought. The more we think our ideas change, the more we reveal the same old beliefs. Increasingly I resented believers who dish out their so-called comfort but succeed in making the sufferer feel condemned, unspiritual, and alone. Increasingly I sensed that they succeeded in comforting themselves alone. I rather despised them. Particularly I despised their belief that they were more spiritual because of the so-called answers. I did not respect their kind of advice.

During those months, I was visited in hospital by a friend Graham, one of the tutors at the college where Matthew was training for the ministry. He arrived late one evening when the ward was quiet and patients around me were beginning to drift off to sleep. His visit cheered me no end, especially as Graham talked of life beyond the confines of my hospital bed.

Before he left, Graham addressed my discouragement which, astute as he was, he had discerned. 'I want to encourage you with a few verses from here,' he said with his steady smile, turning to Romans, chapter 5. 'Is it all right if I read some to you?'

I nodded hopefully.

'"We rejoice in the hope of the glory of God",' he began. I closed my eyes and thought ahead to heaven, secure and therefore content that if I should die, I would be going to a better place. It was exciting indeed to hope for the glory of God. The little niggle which squirmed its way to the surface was that the process of dying was taking so long; I was beginning to be afraid that I might have missed the boat. It felt very much like second best to think that I might be left stranded on earth.

Graham went on. '"Not only so, but we also rejoice in our sufferings . . .".' I could hardly echo that! I didn't positively rejoice in my sufferings! This was beginning to sound like the sort of simplistic religious language which fuelled my irritation at 'comfort' which did not ring true in practice.

'". . . because we know that suffering produces

perseverance; perseverance, character; and character, hope. And hope does not disappoint us, because . . .".'

That was the last straw. I did not want to hear any reasons, theological or philosophical, as to why hope does not disappoint us. It simply didn't ring true, as I blurted out.

'Excuse me, Graham!' I interrupted. 'Hope *has* disappointed me!'

My voice was emphatic, despite my weakness physically, and I'm sure I startled a few patients nearby with my loud voice.

Graham's gaze was thoughtful, listening.

I continued, 'And God has disappointed me!'

Graham's eyes did not leave mine as he listened. I have no idea whether he was shocked or affronted at somebody daring to argue like this.

I was getting the bit between my teeth, pointing with my forefinger on the faded blue bedcover to drive home my words. 'Graham, you surely understand this? We've hoped and we've prayed, and the whole college has done the same. And look at me! I have neither died in peace, nor have I recovered enough to live in peace. Maybe I've grown a little in perseverance, and maybe character too; it's not for me to say. But it's just not true to say that all that has given a new hope which does not disappoint us.'

Graham did not say anything. His face showed no reaction to my tirade, disapproving or otherwise.

I sat back, exhausted yet also exhilarated. Perhaps subconsciously I felt that, in silencing Graham, I must have cornered God whom he represented. Surely I had proved Him wrong.

But as Graham continued to sit there, still saying nothing, my sense of triumph began to fade. Graham was listening. And as the seconds stretched into minutes, I realised that he was listening, not to me, but to God. For some reason, I felt compelled to do the same.

I thank God that Graham did not begin to produce any so-called answers explaining why I was wrong. I was not ready to hear theories or arguments. I knew I sounded belligerent and impertinent to rant as I did. But those were not my motives. The fact was that I needed to offer my honesty to God.

Graham's silence was like a gift to me. In a sense I feel as if I have carried the silence and the listening attitude with me from that evening, through the following months and continuously ever since, for I am still listening now. It is the kind of quiet attitude in which God has room to speak. I have said my piece, and now it's God's turn.

So far I have become aware of two main ways in which I have glimpsed how I was wrong. I say wrong, not naughty, because I am certain that God receives our shouting at Him with much more loving acceptance than humans do. His love, even while we are having our tantrums, is completely patient and kind.

I was wrong first because my hope was focused on what God could do for me. I knew He could heal people physically; I had hoped He would do that for me, and was disappointed because He hadn't. I knew, too, that He could gather dying people into His arms and lead them home to be with Him for ever; I had hoped He would do that for me and was disappointed because He hadn't.

While I clung desperately to what I wanted, I was not giving consideration to Who He was. To concentrate on God Himself, rather than on the blessings He gives, demands a shift in our focus;

it entails an act of will and determination, and a letting go of our wants.

I set about trying to apply familiar aspects of God's nature to my own situation. What exactly *could* I hope in?

I could hope in God's steadfast love which, as He repeated hundreds of times throughout the Bible, never comes to an end. I did not feel the tenderness of His love, but I could hope in it. And then there were His many promises never to leave us nor forsake us; I could hope in them, too.

I turned my mind to God being my Father. That is how He described Himself. I could hope in Him cradling me tenderly as His child. However hurt I felt, I could put the weight of my trust in His fatherhood, if I chose to dwell on that image.

I could hope in Jesus who said He was the Truth. He described Himself as the Light of the world, and as the Good Shepherd, and many other images. I could think on these things, and hope in Him to be these things in my darkness, my lostness.

I could hope in the Holy Spirit, who is described as the Comforter. I could hope in Him being my Comforter. And while I hoped, I would be opening myself to allow for Him to become all these things in me. I began to realise that hoping is not a passive attitude but an activity of making space for God to be Who He is.

This hope would not be for what God could do for me, but in Who He is. Instead of searching for His gifts, I would be looking to the Giver Himself. This is the hope which is not disappointed.

Secondly, I was mistaken because I did not listen to the end of the verse. Such was my awe at the effect of listening to God, copying Graham, I did not take in anything else of Graham's visit. I do not recall any details other than the simple fact that, eventually, he read on. But I was not listening to him any more. It took me some time to come back to those verses in Romans.

However, the passage Graham had chosen to read to me goes on to explain, 'And hope does not disappoint us, because God has poured out his love into our hearts by the Holy Spirit, whom he has given us.'

Years on, I can see that in 1980 when Graham visited me, my prayers were focused on the release I so needed. Unaware of what I was doing, I was actually so busy hoping for God to do something else for me, I was not prepared to look at – never mind appreciate! – what He had already done. I felt much too justified in pointing out where He had apparently failed.

I am not alone in this. Three thousand years ago, in Moses' time, the people of Israel did exactly the same. They also failed to accept God's comfort when He offered it, because they were so busy hoping for more. They were suffering terribly in Egypt under a strict and punitive regime where they were ill-treated and tormented. They prayed for release, just as I did in 1980; they begged God to 'Do something!' and put an end to the futile waste. One day, God drew Moses to one side and spoke His reply, expressing with tenderness and power His understanding and promise. His words are in Exodus 6.

I have heard the groaning of the Israelites . . . I have remembered my covenant. . . . I will bring you out from under the yoke of the Egyptians. I will free you from being slaves to them, and I will redeem you with an outstretched arm . . . I will

take you as my own people, and I will be your God
. . . I will bring you to the land I swore . . . I will
give it to you as a possession. I am the Lord.

But the following verse in the chapter is very sad.
'Moses reported this to the Israelites, but they did
not listen to him because of their discouragement
and cruel bondage.'

I am afraid that I have been just like those
Israelites. I have felt what they felt. Sometimes
our bondage seems so cruel, we do not listen to
whatever God says; we have decided in advance
that He doesn't understand.

It was, unpredictably, through seeing a photograph of something entirely unconnected with anything to do with the Bible that I suddenly recognised
my blinkered vision. A friend was showing me the
photographs of her backpacking tour around the
world and one of the pictures was very powerful.
It was like a parable of my situation.

The photograph was of a valley in New Zealand.
It was stunning: the sweeping glade was ablaze with
colour from a vast meadow of tall lupins. Pinks and
purples and blues of every hue formed a carpet of
abundant life. It was a breathtaking sight.

I found this photograph provocative and unset-
tling. I heard myself wishing, out loud, that I could
be on top of the high, snow-capped mountains
which overlooked the low-lying land. While I was
still speaking, I knew immediately that such a wish
meant that I was prepared to disregard what was in
the valley. Suddenly I felt a sting of shame, for the
valley was so breathtakingly beautiful. How could
I dare to fix my thoughts so determinedly on the
things above that I did not give myself fully to

appreciating the beauty in the valley below? The
realisation brought me once more to my knees.

> If I lift my eyes
> I wish only to be
> high on those hills
>   exhilarated
>   by breathtaking views
>   and by the achievement of arriving

> Open my eyes to where I am, Lord.
> Your carpet of exuberant richness
> is not only above me
> unreachable
> but also beneath my feet
> even when I walk in deep valleys

When we long for something we cannot have, we
may be failing to accept what we have. Mountain
tops are not the only wonderful places to go. Valleys
can be, too.

This was my second mistake while Graham had
tried to read those verses from Romans to me. After
having seen that photograph, I see now that I was
so busy wishing that I were somewhere else, I was
refusing to accept where I was. I was so busy looking
for what else God could do, I was not prepared to
see what He had already done.

The same lesson was brought home to me in a
different way some years later while Matthew was
playing a tape of music from Taizé, in France. This
consisted of simple chants sung by members of a religious community. Matthew and I have enjoyed par-
ticipating in both singing and playing that particular
music, using it during special candlelit services in
church, and we appreciate its value enormously.

The track which Matthew was then playing was as a springboard to prayer: 'Oh Lord, hear my prayer! Oh Lord, hear my prayer! When I call, answer me!'

A minute passed. The soft voices swelled and were more hushed, the beautiful harmonies changed. Two minutes. Always they repeated the same words. 'Oh Lord, hear my prayer! Oh Lord, hear my prayer! When I call, answer me!'

Suddenly after six minutes and still the same few words were repeated, I blurted out, 'I'm quite sure God does hear, you know! In fact, He surely heard the first time.'

Matthew was more involved in the loveliness of the sound to join in with my unexpected quibble. But I explained, 'We pray and we keep pleading for God to answer us, but how *can* He if we won't stop asking Him to listen?!'

During the next track the words of prayer were in Greek. This time there were only three words: 'Kyrie, Kyrie, Eleison.' 'Lord have mercy. Lord have mercy. Lord have mercy.' But the Lord does have mercy! And as I listened to the praying – more objectively than when I myself am praying – I asked myself, how much breath do I spend, begging for God to give me something He has already offered to me? Should my prayers, therefore, be more to do with making myself available to receive what He *does* offer, than beseeching Him to give more?

Perhaps I needed to be disappointed, as I had been, through so many years of illness and apparently unheard prayers, before I was ready to hear, and understand, the subtlety of some of my mistakes. To begin to hear, through the silence, is a treasure indeed. And there is more treasure to discover, if we will listen for more.

5

Life support

I've been dead once already.
It was a very liberating experience.
— Jack Nicholson in *Batman*

I am always inspired to hear and read the stories of people who describe how God has helped them and ministered to them. Often such encounters seem to have been as vital as the life support given by machines in Intensive Care Units. As a nurse I used to look after patients who reached the point when they could not even breathe for themselves. They needed to be relieved of the effort of drawing in their breath, so a ventilator would push air into their lungs for them.

Stories of God coming to people in their crises sound rather like a spiritual version of this. People describe having been at the end of their tether, unable to do anything, when they discovered with elation that God had taken all the effort and breathed His very life into them. All they needed to do was receive from Him. The implication is that, if anyone else longs for such life-giving refreshment, they need only open themselves to receive. If they do not get what they want, they were presumably not available enough.

One of the biggest times of our disappointment in God occurs when we long for God to give us this kind of life support, and He doesn't. We want to depend on the God who cares to impart life to us. We may do all in our power to receive it, and yet not feel any different. The business of trusting Him in the dark becomes dreadfully tedious.

The trouble is that we feel in need of God's life support when, apparently, God does not share our view. He seems to think that we can stand on our own two feet when we feel we can only lie there waiting to be given a spiritual blood transfusion. When we reach the end of our tether, God doesn't always appear too concerned. It's as if He believes we have more tether which merely needs to be pulled out, like those expanding dog-leads. There has to be a tug of pressure before those leads unravel a little more from their hidden store. Sometimes it seems that God doesn't rescue us because He knows our hidden strengths will emerge when a tug of pressure is exerted.

I would like to write reassuringly about God ministering to me whenever I have been in the depths, but that would not be true. What is true is that there have been times when He has, but there have also been times when He has not. One of the hardest aspects of a believer's life is facing, honestly, those times when God has not stepped in to help.

I described one such occasion at the end of *A Pathway through Pain* when, in April 1990, I suddenly plummeted into another episode of acute abdominal pain. All of one night I hung on to life by a thread, my blood pressure falling lower and lower until at about three o'clock in the morning – that low hour before dawn – my kidneys stopped functioning. I was being 'specialled', with a nurse continuously monitoring my breathing, my heartbeat, and watching the various tubes and oxygen all keeping me going. The registrar ordered further steps to try to stop me falling irretrievably down the ravine which was opening ever wider. But my temperature dropped; my pulse raced. Still conscious, I was literally watching my body cease. And on this occasion I felt no peace. No calm assurance of God being with me. I had been overtaken by a terrible mistake which had taken me unawares. It was like a thief which had crept in unseen and was getting away with stealing my life before it could be stopped.

Only one small – so small! – moment brought any relief from the terrible feeling that God had abandoned me. It stands in my memory like a tiny candle (the tiny, little, birthday cake size of candle) flickering its tiny flame of light in a huge cavern of blackness.

A nurse came to clean my mouth. My eyes were closed; she seemed to approach from nowhere. Gently, tenderly, with soft-spoken words, she dabbed her refreshing swab around my gums. Her touch was very soothing. Finally she placed a tiny stick on my lips for a second and let my tongue taste its sweetness. That was it.

I now believe that one mark of angels must be their gentle arrival, unheralded, bringing refreshment and sweetness. They come to our solitude and give just enough for us to survive: no excess. That, when we are *in extremis*, is divine.

Am I suggesting that to be touched by a little stick with glucose is to be visited by an angel? It may have been the timing of such a touch which made it seem angelic. On the brink of death, to be touched on the lips, yes, that is like being given life itself. It makes the difference between the stench of death and the fragrance of life.

It is consolation to think of that nurse that night in hospital being an angel, but actually she was a human, giving what I humanly, physically, needed. To think of this does not actually lessen the dreadfulness of God's intangible nature. Despite that nurse's angelic visit, what I remember from that night is that God did not take away the horror of what was happening. He did not give me His special peace which I had known previously, when I had been just as ill, and I have known since. On that night, He did not give the kind of life support that I desperately wanted from Him.

I do believe that there are angels who minister to us, as they did to Jesus *in extremis*, both in the wilderness after His temptations and in the Garden of Gethsemane before His crucifixion. I don't know whether Jesus recognised them as angels. Certainly I didn't recognise mine. The agony of the night was so great, I was not looking for angels, or blessing – only, desperately, for rescue, for relief: 'Father, take this cup from me . . . I cannot go through with this . . .'

But then, Jesus did not have the benefit of angels ministering to Him until *after* His awful temptations in the wilderness. While the devil was attacking Him, while He was going through the testing time, He was alone. Only later, when Satan had withdrawn, did the angels come. So late! But it seems that God wants us, sometimes, to face life's ruthlessness – His ruthlessness – which we hate and which questions our very faith, and He wants us to make our stand. Even if we quote the words from the Bible rather than use our own, He seems to be pleased to hear us speak out those answers for ourselves. Then He helps us.

We may be afraid of reaching the end of our own resources. For example I am quick to condemn myself if I cease to know how to pray. The implication is that if my spiritual life were truly successful I would do God's will, or try to. I am slow to make provision for times when I might be passive. And so I need to learn how to balance my own activity for Him against the need to make space for God to be active in me.

Let me dare
to stop swimming

to turn on my back

not
in order to drown
uselessly

but
to discover
floating

Let me dare
to stop trying
to do Your will

Let
Your will be done
in me

In Intensive Care Units, patients who are on a life support machine *have* to be passive. If they begin to be active – in other words, if they try to breathe for themselves – they are said to be fighting the ventilator. However, for the life support to be most effective, they must passively receive it. While they need the help of a ventilator, any efforts they make to breathe are knocked out by an injection which paralyses them.

I believe there are occasions when God might want to breathe into us and we may need to stop fighting in order to receive from Him.

Personally, I recall being on a ventilator with a shudder. I felt totally at the mercy of the machine, or the nurse supervising it (I hoped!). As I could not clear my throat for myself, it felt as if I were going to choke whenever a small amount of mucus formed around the tubing down into my windpipe. I was dependent on the nurse to hear what was happening and apply suction to clear my airway. Such dependence on the vigilance of the nurse is a true act of trust. I found it horrifying.

Do we resist such dependence in our spiritual lives as much as we do, naturally, with our breathing? Our fears are reasonable: what if God doesn't hold us totally? What if we fall and He doesn't catch us?

We do have our own life-supporting systems, our defence mechanisms and patterns of behaviour which we have learned from childhood. Defence mechanisms are a vital part of human survival: they literally defend us. We may be unaware of our need to change our own strategies and exchange them for God's type of support. Yet if a time comes when God seeks to minister to us, my experience is that He asks us to lower our own defences. To say 'Yes' to Him, then, is to allow Him in to where we feel most vulnerable, where none have entered before. It is natural for us to be afraid of yielding so much to Him. Surrender is a daring process.

It is easy to want God's help; it is hard to abandon what is familiar. It is hard to give up our defences. In my case, I felt as if one of my defences was torn from me. I felt God had been torn from me. I needed to learn – and I still give time to keep on learning – how to accept God's kind of comfort, of soothing, of being beside and staying beside. I needed to learn that He does not condemn weakness.

This was unfamiliar to me. While I was growing up, I decided that the safest strategy to adopt when something hurt me was for me to say that it wasn't sore. That way, I ensured that I defended myself against two possibilities which I definitely wanted to avoid: being mocked for being a 'cry-baby', or being smothered with the kind of concern which burdened me more than it helped me.

I guess that my environment also confirmed my strategy. If I fell over and hurt myself I was told, 'It's not sore!' or, 'It's all better now!' If it was sore, I was puzzled, torn between believing what I felt and what the grown-ups said (and their voices were the ones I was taught to obey). If it didn't feel 'better now', I blamed myself. I concluded that I must be a baby to feel pain when grown-ups told me there was none. Very early in life I chose to deny pain, even – especially – to myself. To do that brought me a measure of comfort.

I had not let go of this childhood behaviour when I became ill as an adult. When pain struck, several days after my initial appendix operation, I used my well-practised defence against it, assuring myself and the doctors that it was 'not too sore'. Whatever happened, I wanted to avoid moaning more than was acceptable. I quoted the same words I had learned while still a baby, that I *was* better, when I wasn't. My strategy didn't work and I tried harder. When the signs and symptoms clearly took over and I could no longer deny how I was, I felt abandoned by God. Only now, fifteen years afterwards and with specific help, do I see that I was actually abandoned not by God but by familiar comfort. And only when I looked objectively at that familiar 'comfort' did I see that it had actually not been comforting at all.

Perhaps sometimes our fear of being abandoned by God is a fear that we may need to abandon some of our childhood patterns of behaviour and reactions. Deep down, we know that if God is worth anything at all, He will not abandon us. So we know that, if we feel deserted, or alone, that feeling is coming from something else, something hidden. We can remain afraid until we look into the darkness we most fear, to explore what is the true source of our fear. To do so is horrifying. It is also the most reassuring thing we can do, for we discover for ourselves the truth which is repeated so often throughout the Bible. God is always with us. We cannot be separated from His love. Even demons cannot come between us and God's love. Our fears are a deceit; a huge, lying deceit. We need never be afraid.

Where does my confidence to write this come from? I attribute it to an occasion many years ago now, when the blinkers were lifted from my vision. This was not something I achieved. I was passive. The only way I can describe it is by saying that God visited me.

It was 1984 and I was living in Beverley. Before the night which was to be so special, I had gone through a terrible crisis of claustrophobia. I had realised with horror that I was trapped in a prison of pain. Having pinned my hopes that the whole saga of my recurring illness would end completely with the 'total pelvic clearance' – such a radical operation including a hysterectomy when I was only twenty-four years old – I was devastated when, three years later, I was not only back in hospital but going back for yet more major abdominal surgery. I felt I could not face it.

My inability to escape the situation hit me with particular force when the nurses had finished preparing me for theatre. They opened the curtains around my bed, and I noticed them tick me off their list. They could proceed to the next patient. I had to stay where I was. And at that moment, as the curtains swung to rest and I looked out on the rest of the ward, I felt most terribly alone.

I had been expected to face the world and to cope, but I felt I could not. I had been expected to go through with so many, such severe episodes of pain, and so much surgery, but I had exhausted my resources of courage. I felt I had no so-called bravery left. I could not face being so ill again. Yet there was no escape. I simply had to ride the storm for as long as I remained in this body. I felt completely trapped.

A lady in the bed beside me looked across at me. Seeing the tears falling silently down my cheeks she must have concluded that I was nervous of an operation.

'Poor dear,' she muttered to her neighbour in a voice as near to a whisper as old ladies seem to manage. 'She's young to be having all this done to her.'

But that was not it. It was not my young age that made it so hard. I could have explained, had I had the inclination, that I had had more – much more – than this at a 'young age'! But what was the point of any explanations? Can those alongside understand all about me? My history? Of course not, any more than I could understand all about the hidden pain they faced.

No. It was not my age that I could not bear; nor even our human inability to understand one another fully. It was the relentlessness of the whole situation, the fact that my illness just kept on and on with its relentless course. And for what purpose? It all seemed so futile. Surely, if there had been lessons to learn, I had learned them by now?

Overwhelmed by the powerlessness of being unable to escape, I buried my head under the starched hospital sheet. With rising panic I found myself considering ripping out all the tubes and running away.

'No, Lord. I can't; I can't; I CAN'T!'

At that very second Matthew walked through the door. His time as a curate was flexible, allowing him to drop in to see me whenever he chose. His face was calm and his eyes warmly loving.

'Matthew, I can't have another operation!' I blurted out before he had even reached my bed and said hello. He came over and lifted my clenched hand into both of his.

'I can't face it. Not another!'

'I know.' Matthew's eyes showed little expression behind his glasses.

'Matthew, don't you understand?' I persisted in my panic. 'This is more than I can bear!'

He did understand. It was more than he could bear, too, to watch me suffer. But he did not consider the hurt to himself foremost. He just looked at me kindly and repeated, 'I know, my lady.'

Perhaps his caring touch stemmed the flow of my panic a little. I do not know. What I remember is that he said, 'Let's pray', and before I was able to argue he had asked God to be with me, to be beside me, and to comfort me.

In the midst of my human fear in that awful hour, I was slow to acknowledge any answer to Matthew's prayer. Somehow I found composure enough to go through with the inevitable surgery. But such was the intensity of the situation, for a while I was completely taken up fighting the battles within. It took me some time to register also the peace which grew from that very fight.

Certainly I still felt far from peaceful on the night, four or five days after the operation. I was at the awful in-between stage of recovery: not yet well, but aware that I had improved, not least because I had been promoted from an intensive care bed to a position half way down the ward. The operation had been a success and I was certainly out of danger. But I was not yet better enough to be comfortable.

I tossed restlessly in the bed, trying to sleep first in one position on my side and then another on my back. I longed to enjoy the release brought by sleep. But I was not at peace. I knew I had not prayed – at least, not formally – during those intervening days. For some of that time I had been unconscious in Intensive Care, on a ventilator – of course my prayer life had suffered! Nevertheless I also knew (but did not want to admit) that I did not want to pray. To do so would have meant opening myself to the possibility of relinquishing my anger, and I did not want to do that. It felt justified. Thus an unwelcome sense of guilt added to my restlessness; the kind of guilt which is effective at inhibiting prayer.

I lay with this prickling discomfort, unable to reason away my feelings. And suddenly, without warning, I was aware of God with me. He was beside me.

My breath was almost taken away from me. Such closeness with God was all the more disarming because it was unexpected. I had not been in a 'proper' attitude of prayer, and nor (if I was honest) had I wanted to be. Yet now it was as if every cell in my body was being diffused with His peace. Whatever was happening to me, I knew this was God.

I wondered whether I was about to see Jesus in person. His presence was so real that I would not have been surprised. I longed to see Him. I hoped He might come and sit on my bed (the way nurses tell one not to do!) and take my hand. I thrust my hands outside the covers to ensure that they were ready, if His presence should become visible.

Then I heard my name being called. It was not so much a voice which I could describe, or imitate; rather my name seemed to hang on the air – 'Jane'. It conveyed to me that God knew everything about me. It was also an invitation. It reminded me immediately of the young boy, Samuel, who heard God calling him in the night. I wanted to use my voice in reply, as Samuel had been instructed to do. However, I was still aware of the other patients in the ward and I did not want them to overhear me, so I merely whispered my reply, 'Speak, Lord, for your servant is listening.'

God did not speak with an audible voice. Simply, His Being was with me. That was what spoke. And He was so big! So much bigger than I had imagined! His presence filled the night. I recall the flash of realisation, 'If only we knew You were this big, Lord, our questioning and doubts would be silenced . . .'

Gradually, the special burning immanence of God began to fade. He had been so close, it seemed only logical that there would be some physical sign of the power of His presence.

My first thought was that my wound would be healed: not just improved, but that there would be no wound at all. No scar. No stitches. The whole experience had been so miraculous, I would not have been surprised. God had been so big, I knew such a miracle would have been a doddle for Him. I slipped one hand under the covers of my bed. Gently, I began to peel back the bandage down one side. Gingerly, slowly, I eased my finger down the side of the dressing to feel for the familiar shape of the stitches. I swallowed. I could identify the dried blood caked all around.

Unwilling to believe what my fingertips told me, I lifted the blankets a few inches and peered through the darkness. The light was very subdued in the dim ward, but I had been awake for so long, my eyes were accustomed to the darkness. I opened the little slot of white dressing which I had loosened. My heart seemed to thud more loudly.

The stitches were there. Ugly, black and oozing with pus. I replaced the covering.

How could there be no miracle, when God had been so close to me?

No sooner had the question formed in my mind than the glow of God's presence pulsed through me once again. My puzzlement subsided as rapidly as it had arrived. The overwhelming conviction which had been imparted to me was immovable. My wound was unchanged, but I was not. I had an unquestioning certainty that, whatever God wanted to do with my life or my body, He was with me. He was to be trusted.

The following day, still elated by the wonder at God visiting me in such an extraordinary way, I wrote to some friends who had been praying for me. I wanted to reassure them that the unpleasantness of my suffering had paled into insignificance. I wrote of my conviction that there are seeds within pain – hidden seeds. I knew God would bring fruit from my pain although I recorded, 'Of course I do not know that I will ever see it.' I had no idea, then, of how much I would need to hold on to that assurance.

That night I knew, through glimpsing the greatness of God's presence, that my suffering was not a terrible mistake. I began to accept it as being under the fatherly hand of God. He was in control. We can believe in the goodness of God. Since that night, I have never had any doubt of that.

We can fear being at the end of our rope a little less. We can trust God's grace to be there, in our most feared darkness, a little more.

It may sound very lame, but sometimes I forget my experience of God visiting me as He did in hospital. I see what is near me and not what is beyond. I need to learn how to look behind the horror of continued suffering and I need to keep learning, with every episode of pain, how to touch God in the depths.

I used to think that if I had a wonderful enough

experience of God I would be satisfied. Now I see that that is not true. No matter how delicious a taste we have had of God, it's only ever a foretaste. It's not the full banquet. To feel the touch of God does satisfy completely for that moment, that day, but on the morrow we find ourselves wanting it again, wanting Him again, wanting more of Him. This is not a failure on our part. It is still blessed to keep knowing our need of God.

In Moses' day, when the Israelites were crossing the desert after they had crossed the Red Sea, they became hungry. God gave them food – manna – every day, sustaining them, giving them both physical and spiritual support. They were dependent on God to provide this manna each day. They had to accept His sustenance while it was fresh, for that one day only. He gave insufficient for two days; indeed, if they tried to collect more than one day's ration the manna went stale (except at weekends!). I see this as a picture of one fact which I am slow to accept. God's sustenance does go stale if I try to store it rather than partake of it. I will be disappointed if I try to feed today on yesterday's gift. It seems that God likes us to be dependent on Him, and daily. This is something I might wish to grow out of as I grow towards independence, but which I am learning to grow into as I grow towards Him.

This journey towards dependence is one which we are all invited to make. It is a journey of which death is a part, if we are ever to give up our old ways and be surprised and enthralled by resurrection.

In my experience, this kind of death often occurs at night, when I am alone. I may have longed for others to show me more care during the day, but they had proved unable to fulfil all my wants, even if they

had been willing to try. Then I have been left, alone
– or rather, alone with God. It sounds quite hateful,
but it is in fact a blessed, blessed place to be: deserted
by friends who, in our folly, we believed could help
us more than our naked encounter with God.

> When I cling to what I want
>   I am heading only towards death
> When I dwell on what hurts me
>   I allow myself to be more hurt
> When I harbour grudges against those
>   who do not understand me
>   I close a door to forgiveness
> Or I shrink back from giving
>   a silent gesture of love
>   a quiet word of reassurance
>   Then I strangle compassion
>   stifling its growth
>   choking its breath
>
> But You Who are Life,
> The One Who revives,
>   You do not leave me choking
>
> You come to me
>   Offering the moment
>   When more of myself
>   can be made alive
>   in You
>
> You come to me
>   Offering the moment
>   When more of Yourself
>   can be made alive
>   in me

6

Hide 'n' heal?

Seeds need to be buried, watered,
and kept in a dark place if they are
to germinate
— a gardener

Pain hidden is not pain healed. Hiding may be a temporary escape, but whenever we close our minds to what hurts us we also shut out an area where God is waiting to be found.

No-one would ever have guessed that a nursing colleague of mine, Rachel, knew pain so deeply as she did. Perhaps we should have recognised that she was able to understand and draw alongside her patients in a particular way. Had I had more maturity in my days as a student nurse, I might have recognised that the quality of compassion which was natural to Rachel had grown with much struggle from seeds within her pain.

Rachel had been fun to work with on the wards, and bright in college. Throughout our years of training together, she did outstandingly well. But she was deeply distressed by praise. When nominated as 'Nurse of the Year', she declined vehemently to stand for election.

Looking back I see now that she had been more than just self-effacing. There was a trace of tension and of fear. It was as if she were afraid that praise was all a mean joke which could only hurt her. She was unable to trust others. Tears would fill her eyes and we knew not to press her to tell us what was wrong. In fact she dismissed praise so totally that, by the time she was about thirty, she was overwhelmed by the feeling that her life had no value at all. She became suicidal.

Once, and only once, Rachel poured out her heart in a letter from abroad. She wrote that she had been hurt as a child, so much so that she had vowed never to talk about it. She knew that the wounds she carried must filter into her adult life. But her resolve was to keep the past behind her. She dared not begin to explore her hurts lest they return to haunt her overwhelmingly again. She did acknowledge, however, that her hurts were hidden rather than healed.

Mark was very different from Rachel. When he came up to me at the end of a meeting he did so with studied reluctance.

'I wish I'd never come here,' he rued. He set his shoulders. 'I need God to take me out of this dreadful situation, and He can't.' He was sure that his situation was so grim that the only way God could possibly help was by rescuing him from it.

He began to tell of his pain, giving more and more details and barely pausing for breath. He gave no time for reflection, although he did make strategic halts at those most emotional parts of his story which lent themselves to expressions of pity. His barrage of words was very different from Rachel's silence.

Or was it? The more Mark talked, the less worthwhile I felt our discussion to be. He could talk about hurt, yes, but as his tale went round and round, I sensed that he was touching only the periphery. I watched his face as he dangled his lurid details before me, waiting for my exclamations of sympathy. He seemed untouched even by the most pitiful things he was saying. Was he unable to face his pain? Was he using words to avoid thinking about what really hurt him?

Rachel used her suffering to resource her to give others the care she longed to have received herself. Mark was not able to reach out to others yet. He expressed great discomfort at the idea that others suffer, too. He believed that pain singled him out.

'Everyone tries to help,' he said. 'But their so-called answers are never right for me.'

I flinched. How many people like Mark had I unconsciously offended as I had tried to 'help' them?

The easiest way of coping would have been to blame him for being too selfish. Rather desperately that evening I wondered how Jesus would have shown His love. Certainly, any 'answers' would have seemed intolerable without Mark seeing the compassion in Jesus's eyes.

Was it to people such as this that Jesus told His parables about yeast? Only a tiny amount was needed, Jesus said, to cause a whole batch of heavy dough to be raised into light bread. Would He have promised Mark that he would be transformed when the Holy Spirit diffused him with new life?

Maybe Jesus would have been moved with

compassion to touch Mark and heal him, as He did the woman who was physically crippled?

Or would Jesus have grieved over Mark's stubborn self-pity, saying, 'If you had only known on this day what would bring you peace! . . . You did not recognise the time of God's coming to you!' (Luke 19:42, 44). But He would not have spoken thus in judgment. As over Jerusalem, He would have been weeping – not impotent tears because there was nothing He could do. Jesus's tears were shed because He knew He could help.

Mark, however, had closed himself off from every kind of help. He could not understand when I spoke to him of Jesus's tears. 'If Jesus felt so upset about me,' he argued, 'He would use His power to help me out of this mess.' He told me he had to reject God. He was very bitter. He could not see that a bit of him hung back from receiving help; a bit of him seemed to want to hug his hurt, to nurture and protect it. His grief had become his grievance. Curled as he was around himself, he was afraid to risk being uncurled.

I came home that night feeling drained and dejected. I had allowed myself to be dragged into becoming the victim instead of the carer. Mark was refusing to let anyone, let alone God, in to where he truly hurt, and while he did so no treasures could ever be seen. His pain was only negative.

The carer as a victim

I could not condemn Mark. The compassion of others is a relief at first and I have sought it myself. Occasionally I, too, have 'confided' in others, telling myself that I was merely obeying others' advice.

But I have known deep down when I have been indulging in more than sharing facts with them. I have interpreted events to conform to my own bitter outlook. I have wanted to convey to others my sense of oppression as well. I have wanted my friends to feel oppressed with me, as if to prove to me that they care.

Whenever I allow myself such indulgent luxury, I lose any sense of God's healing. I feel alone. For others' pity slips through the soul as through a sieve, leaving a bitterness more stark than before. Then I want others to join me in feeling sorry for me. I say that I want them to pray for me; actually I want them to feel for me too. I demand too much. I allow my suffering to impose on others more than they are able to bear. I get it wrong. I am tempted to pooh-pooh others' pain and say (to myself, if not out loud) that theirs is not as bad as mine.

Whenever I look at how grim I feel, I want to point to myself. That is not facing up to my pain. It is hiding. It is refusing to accept it, and thereby refusing to accept God in it.

This leads me to identify a third way of rejecting God, and rejecting others; a way which is a subtle trick of which we are rarely conscious. It took time and insight into my own ugly ways before I could see that what masquerades as bravery can actually be a game we play, in which the carer is made into a victim.

Yvonne would never have moaned in pain. She was tight-lipped and quiet but at church we knew she was unwell, yet she insisted repeatedly, 'No, I'm fine!' We would catch sight of her when pain was engraved in creases across her face yet she rejected our help. I thought that she had immense courage.

One evening I offered her a lift home but she refused. Later I heard that she had fainted during her stagger home. When speaking to the doctor the following day I mentioned how guilty I felt that Yvonne had lain alone and in pain. And that was when the doctor raised her hand to refute me.

'No, Jane,' she said. 'That's a trap, you know. It's set up to make the carer a victim.'

She explained that what was happening in this instance was a power game. A patient knows that the carer cares; by rejecting help she ensures that love is given no avenue for expression. The carer is then left, dangling, holding on to impotence. The patient feels a subtle power. She has caused someone to share her suffering, to share the impotence. And she holds the keys to the power.

I write 'she' because, in my experience, women are much more adept at playing this game. Men who feel terrible are usually much easier to please – certainly for a nurse. They usually accept any care offered, in an almost child-like way. They love to have their fevered brow mopped, and they don't mind having such a gesture repeated long after the fever has gone! Women, however, of whom I am no exception, are different. We can use devious ways. We can act out bravery giving an entirely credible picture of courage-in-the-face-of-awful-circumstances, when internally we feel martyrs. We can 'share' dark clouds of our experience while internally reassuring ourselves of the silver lining which we may never disclose to the listener. We know things we do not say. We hold this reassurance and we use it as a power which we will not give away. This causes the carer to be a victim.

I write this at length because the true carer is

Jesus. We can try to make Him into our victim.
If we entrench ourselves in our position of being
unhelpable, we render Him impotent – or rather,
we convince ourselves that that is so.

Yet Jesus enters our dark and horrible and
stinking places just as He entered the stable in
Bethlehem. That was His birthplace two thousand
years ago and it can be His birthplace daily within
us. His name Emmanuel means 'God with us'.
God-With-Us entered a shameful place among
dung and, without 'doing' anything, He caused
shepherds to recognise God and worship Him there.
At times His way is, still, to make His presence
known to us right where we are, among whatever
causes us shame.

> You've been born in my life
> You're welcome
> And I've decorated the place
> for You to come in
> and with tinsel, and lights, and music
> I celebrate Your birth in me

> > But You came
> > not to the place which is light
> > but into the dark places
> > Into a hidden stable
> > at the back

> > And You ask
> > to be born today
> > in my dark places
> > my hidden areas
> > in the recesses of my being
> > among the dung of my life
> > where no preparation is made

You want it lit
not by my festive candles
but by the single flame
of Your life beginning
even in that stench

And I'm told of Your glory
by angels announcing
that You have crept in

So I dare to look
into the backyard of my heart
And I worship You

A young woman once wrote to me after reading *A Pathway through Pain*, saying, 'There are bits inside us all that we are ashamed of, don't like, don't want anyone else to see. We don't want to look at them ourselves, and we pretend those bits are not there. The last thing we want to do is come straight out with it and give it to God, and look for Him there. Let's not admit to the nasty dark bits! To give ourselves totally to God: how many people really know what this means?'

But here is a key to our healing. There are seeds within pain, and we will hide from these, too, if we refuse to explore the dynamics of persistent or repeated pain. Seeds need to be sown, otherwise they remain dry and useless and they cannot germinate.

Seeds to sow

Psalm 126, written in the face of heartfelt suffering, says, 'He who goes out weeping, carrying seed to sow, will return with songs of joy, carrying sheaves with him.' There is something deliberate about this sowing: sowing our suffering in God, sowing our tears in Him. It is to act more positively than simply to say, 'Time heals'. It demands that we be more bold with our suffering than our culture suggests we can be, or should be.

How do we sow these seeds which we trust to be present in our suffering, but cannot see? We must put our experience into the right environment. Soil is the environment for sowing plant seeds; prayer is the environment for sowing the seeds within our suffering.

When Jesus reached out to touch God in His darkness in Gethsemane, His prayer changed from His initial pleading. He changed from telling His Father that the suffering was more than He could bear. He came to offer Himself unreservedly into His Father's hands.

I take comfort that it is often through praying 'wrong' words that we move on to this type of prayer. Prayer is not our words: it is God's work. Through whatever words we use, prayer is a process of abandoning ourselves to God, into His hands, His way, His guidance. It entails self-sacrifice to yield what we want. When we seek His face, our desire for an end to our suffering is replaced by a growing desire for God.

We cannot bring glory to God through our successes or our brokenness, but God can. He can when we give ourselves into His hands – no matter what state we are in.

> Tonight,
> while pain increases
> and nausea too
> it's like

a huge wave
rising high above me
till it towers over me

And I am afraid
because I know
it could crash down on me
(it has before)

and my head will reel
with the pounding of foaming froth
and the weight of water

This may overcome me one day!

But I'll ask You, Lord,
    to help me to ride
    across this wave
    which curls around with menace

And I'll picture those surfers
    who are not afraid
    but who ride big waves:
    reigning the power of the water
    to propel them
    to new places

And I'll take Your hand
    and, balancing,
I'll be held in Your power
    which is perfected in weakness

So I'll be led to new places
    Your goals
where You will have done new work

And I can rest again
in the eddies of Your shelter.

Seeds are hidden in darkness underground: they need to be so in order to germinate. I am coming to believe that the darkness which is essential to the natural world may be vital to our spiritual growth. Our experience of pain could be a necessary environment for the growth of those seeds which we neither see nor, possibly, even know about. We may spend our time feeling a sense of loss, grieving, looking for meaning but not finding it. To find the seeds is as hard as finding tiny black dots in the garden soil.

We can be so blinded by what we cannot see or do not understand, we doubt that God is doing anything other than ignoring our plight. Yet God did much of His important work in darkness. When He gave Moses the ten commandments, He did so not in a clear atmosphere but when the mountain was shrouded in fog. Moses had to have the courage to 'approach the thick darkness where God was' (Exodus 20:21). When God guided the children of Israel across the desert, He led them with a cloud. Even the resurrection happened at night, before the darkness lifted. Even if we can see nothing of Him, God does His creative and important work in our darkness, too.

7

Touching God in the depths

*It would be just another illusion to believe
that reaching out to God
will free us from pain and suffering. Often, indeed,
it will take us where we would rather not go.*
                                    – Henri Nouwen

When we are in the depths we are cut off – cut
off from familiar comforts, from others. Sometimes
we cannot admit the depths of our despair to those
we love and who love and fear for us. We feel
desperately alone, isolated, possibly deserted by
others. We may feel cut off even from ourselves.

Perhaps it is exactly the aloneness of our suffering
which acts as a catalyst to our faith and enables us to
look to God. When my illness became a long-term
situation, rather than an event, I felt I was stranded
miles away from anybody familiar. The longer it
went on, the more difficult the aloneness became.
I could have been in an igloo in the middle of
the Antarctic somewhere, so completely cut off
was I from normal life. In those kind of depths,
an instinctive wish is to touch God.

It's like an Arctic hibernation
Pain

When summer's fun
stops
waiting to resume
after winter's finished
and the sun will rise again

Like a sentence
in an igloo

Where reality is
distant
Except, of course, for pain
Which blocks out all else
Like a thick drift of snow

    Have the nights to grow yet longer
    ere the thaw will come?

Others' words are
muffled
absorbed by the snow
My cries sound all the louder
entrenched within this hole

Winter is worsening
Outside hope is not yet

Into this hibernation, Come, Lord:
    Be my flame
    my warmth
    my light
    my hope!

As soon as we stop hiding from our hurt and become
willing to accept and explore it, we begin to reach

out for God. Of all the reasons why people pray, or ask others to pray for them, the most common stems from the longing to touch God when they need help.

There are times when we reach out to touch God in our depths and we are more aware of reaching than of touching. In my own experience this has felt all the more disappointing when I have prayed in a crisis and it has seemed as if my prayers have touched a void rather than the powerful God I have sought. One such occasion was when, although I had been whisked quickly into hospital, I was still hoping that this was not a specially serious episode and that I would, therefore, avoid any treatment which was too traumatic.

'May I have a sip of water?' I asked the nurse as she flicked the crisply laundered covers over me, smoothing her stylish corner. Having to ask for even the simplest requirement like a sip of water represented the dependence and vulnerability I loathed about being made into a patient. Tubes had been stuck into me, injections given to me – strong ones which blurred my whole mind. At last, after hours of being prodded and poked and X-rayed and discussed in the admissions unit, I was being settled into a bed in the ward.

'Sorry,' she replied, but without any regret in her voice. 'You're probably going to theatre.'

Theatre! Her words struck into me. I could hardly manipulate my dry tongue to question her more.

'What, tonight?' I blurted out, more in an attempt to delay her from rushing off than to voice my shock. This was news to me.

The nurse looked me over as if I were stupid. 'Yes,' she said curtly. 'Didn't you know?' And without waiting for a reply she marched off. She looked as if she put more care into the swagger of her hips than she did into comforting those who were hurting.

She could not have guessed the effect of her words on me. I could not face another operation. *Could* not! How many times had I been to theatre – twenty? As in Beverley (chapter 5), my mind raced ahead, as if flicking quickly through a series of photographs. But, alone in the darkness, I relived the horror of each of those moments with a vividness which astonished me.

Already I could envisage the simplistic explanations by nurses too caught up in routines to know either that I had gone through this so often before, or that as a nursing Sister I had been the one to teach nurses such as themselves to help other patients through similar times. And I could envisage now the long road to recovery, the gaping loss of strength, the insidious lowering of spirits. In the silence of the dark ward, with the steady drip of the intravenous infusion as the only movement I could see, I wanted to escape from such a possibility – not to be flung into it, alone.

I tossed about restlessly in bed. There was nothing I could do. I was completely helpless, unable to take control of events happening to me. I felt utterly taken over. Bound and entwined by pain again, stuck in that bed if not by the tubes attached to me then by the pain itself . . . Perhaps it was only in the loneliness of the long night that I was forced to face up to my own reactions. The truth was that I would have done anything in my power to avoid accepting the pathway through pain on which I found myself.

'I hate this!' I cried in the quietness of the dark

ward. 'I hate this, Lord!' I repeated, as if to prove to myself that it was God whom I was addressing.

The steady drip of the intravenous infusion continued its silent course. Nothing else moved, or changed. Still I was alone in my anguish.

Did it matter to God that I felt unable to face more surgery? I had always trusted that His plans were for the best – better even than my own – and Sarah's experience over the death of her son had given any encouragement I may have needed. But at times like this it seemed that He disregarded the wretchedness of enduring tedious, relentless, pointless pain.

Why did God not rescue me? It seemed that He was doing exactly the reverse. He was allowing my suffering to continue. I stared up at the bag of fluid feeding into my arm. Vacantly I tried to read its black writing, but my eyes refused to focus. The injection's effect was stronger than my efforts. Once more I felt taken over by events bigger than I could master.

I determined not to give in. I tried to instruct myself against self-pity. I resolved not to become despondent. But I was swimming against the tide, and the tide was so strong, I knew I needed more support than I could muster for myself.

I decided to look for help in one of the psalms. Perhaps that would help me to be inspired by how other people, more godly than I, had prayed when faced with onslaughts such as my own that night.

Clumsily, with my arm bandaged and splinted around its intravenous tube, I reached for my Bible and turned to Psalm 27. This one, I knew, began full of hope for exactly the kind of help which I wanted from God: 'The Lord is my light and my salvation – whom shall I fear?'

I gazed through this first verse, struggling not only

to read but also to comprehend. Certainly I wanted
that sentiment to be true. I knew God was my light
and salvation, and I wanted to believe that I had
no-one else to fear because of His goodness. But at
that moment, quite honestly, my trust in Him did
not put an end to my fear. I could have answered
that question, 'Whom shall I fear?' with one word:
Surgeons!

I repeated my instruction to myself to guard
against self-pity. I read on:

> When evil men advance against me to
>   devour my flesh
> [this was suitably graphic, I thought!]
> when my enemies and my foes attack me,
>   they will stumble and fall.

If only this were true! If only God gave grand,
sweeping decrees which put an end to our enemies!
Perhaps I did not need quite such a dramatic end to
the surgeons as the psalm suggested literally (though
the idea did make me chuckle), but certainly I did
have several other enemies which I wanted God to do
away with as sweepingly as possible . . . the pain, the
sickness, the loneliness of suffering without comfort.
If only God would put an end to these!

But He was not doing so. He had not intervened.
I had to face what I found impossible.

I dragged my thoughts back to the psalm, beginning to scan it rather than read it verse by verse. I
didn't like the fact that it wasn't ringing true for
me. I was intent on searching for the kind of hope
in God that I could take hold of for myself:

'For in the day of trouble
He [God] will keep me safe . . .'

This was my 'day of trouble' all right – and it had stretched to a night of trouble also. But would God keep me safe? I knew He wouldn't necessarily protect me from having to go through more surgery: I had asked Him to do that before, and He hadn't. He had helped me in other ways, but not that.

'He will hide me in the shelter of his tabernacle . . .'

Would He? But being crippled by pain isn't being hidden in His shelter! I *wanted* this sort of protection, but circumstances caused me to feel exposed, and raw; not sheltered.

'And set me high upon a rock . . .'

Where was this rock? The point was, I could not rise above these circumstances. No amount of faith would let me avoid the fact that I had been dragged into terrible events. God was not lifting me up out of them.

I pushed my Bible away from me, down on to my knees, away from the pain. Was I supposed to be comforted to read of others, like this psalmist, certain of being rescued by God, when I could not share such conviction? This psalm was not helping me in the way I wanted. I was looking for comfort which it didn't give. I could not share the same pious words to God as this psalmist. I could not praise God for rescuing me from my enemies.

I began to feel rather cynical. I did not want to read of promises which seemed unlikely to be fulfilled in me. Any hopes I might secretly have had for a spectacular miracle that night were dwindling. They seemed only naïve fantasies now; castles in the air which symbolised my failure to accept how physically disordered my body had become.

And God was not changing anything. Still, the

only movement visible was the silent drip of my intravenous infusion. Did God realise how hard His non-intervention was for us mortals to bear? The coldness of hard facts to accept; it was like being given a stone.

As I allowed my cynicism room to expand, I recalled how Jesus had talked about stones, making life – and prayer in particular – sound pretty straightforward and easy. 'Which of you, if his son asks for bread, will give him a stone?' Lying that night in hospital, I felt as if God had done that. Exactly that. I had asked for bread – to be freed from pain – and He had given me a stone – more pain.

I knew the passage quite well where Jesus had been talking about bread and stones. 'Ask, and it will be given to you,' He had said. It was all part of His Sermon on the Mount. He had told everyone that we could trust our heavenly Father to give us good things, even more than we could trust our own fathers.

Anger rose in me; anger that Jesus had been so full of assurance about God giving us good things whenever we asked for them. Why had He assured us like that at all? Why had He not added the word, 'usually' if it were not always true? I wanted to trust God, but Jesus's easy-sounding formula did not stand up to the test of some circumstances. It was simply not true that He would necessarily rescue me from an operation just because I asked Him to: He hadn't before, not once, but all too many times. I had trusted Him then. Now His words sounded like an empty promise.

I loathed to find myself resentful about God's promises. I wanted to believe them at face value, but in this situation these words hurt rather than comforted. The events spoke more loudly than His words.

And then, into my swirling mind came another memory about stones. Jesus had once been surrounded by hard stones. It had happened in the wilderness when He was tempted; indeed, the very first temptation was to change stones into bread in order to give Himself what He wanted. Jesus had wanted the same as I did: something nice, and warm, and comforting, instead of something cold and hard and horrid. But His response was to say no, that was wrong. That would be using God's power the wrong way, for selfish ends. He did have God's power but, He said, it was more important to accept what God gives us than to start hankering after changing it into something we find more attractive.

If it was wrong for Jesus to use God's power for His own ends, did this mean it was also wrong for me? Should I, too, be looking for God within that horrid, hard situation? Was I to stop asking Him to change it and, instead, feed on Him right where I was? Was the idea of using God's power for myself actually a temptation which I needed to resist?

I felt drawn to pick up the Bible once more and persevere. I still yearned to share the same hope for God's help as the psalmist. Before reading, I cried, 'God, I need You to set me on a safe rock most of all at times like now!'

Through blurred and watery eyes I forced myself to read on. A little farther down the page I saw,

> One thing I ask of the Lord,
>   this is what I seek:
> that I may dwell in the house of the Lord
>   all the days of my life . . .

My conscience pricked. I was asking Him for only 'one thing', but it was not that I would live in His presence. I was asking Him for something very different. Almost singlemindedly, that night, I was asking to be freed from pain.

I swallowed rather guiltily, but fortunately, guilt did not prevent me from reading on. Still the page gripped me. Only a few lines down the page, three words caught my eye.

'Seek His face!'

The words stirred something deep within me. Here was the kind of instruction which was more of an invitation than a guilt-inducing command. That phrase, quite simply, summarised God's hope for us. It encapsulated very clearly why He had created us, His children. This was His heartfelt desire, and that verse revealed what He wants us to do in our lives.

I fiddled uncomfortably with my drip tube. I had to concede that I must be failing basically in the way I prayed for things. When I sought God I did so as much for what He could do for me as for who He was.

I sighed and looked back over the years. God had not rescued me from recurrent illness. Yet I could not deny that He had been with me through it all. He may not have changed the events, but He had changed me because He was holding me through them.

Could that have been what the psalmist meant at the beginning of his psalm, I wondered? I glanced back to the beginning:

> The Lord is my light and my salvation –
>   whom shall I fear?
> The Lord is the stronghold of my life . . .

Perhaps I could say the same. Without God's light, I would have had no idea of how to reach for Him, to touch Him in the depths. Without His Spirit, I would certainly have had no stronghold at all. The horror of being told of this next possible operation could have been an all-consuming despair.

A flicker of new understanding dawned on me. Despair. Yes, I thought to myself. *That's* my real enemy. More than the abdominal pain which takes over my body. Despair eats into my very soul.

I began to sense that this psalm could relate to me after all. Instead of thinking of my enemies as surgeons, or pain, doing nasty things *to* me, should I think of them as despair which does nasty things *in* me?

I looked back to the top of the page again:

> When my enemies and foes attack me,
>   they will stumble and fall . . .
> Though an army besiege me,
>   my heart will not fear.

Suddenly I saw that suffering was not my worst enemy. My enemies were those things which crept unseen into my soul and fed despair. They were the ugly things like self-pity, resentment, bitterness, pride or denial. Anything which stops us from seeking His face is our enemy. And God could 'keep me safe' from them. He could 'hide me in His shelter' away from them. He could 'set me high upon a rock' above them. How? He causes the real enemies to be rendered harmless whenever I seek His face.

'Then my head will be exalted, above the enemies who surround me.' My head had not been lifted above physical pain. But even while I had been reading that psalm, even through anger and frustration and loathsome emotional reactions, God had addressed my mind and lifted my head above my real enemies.

Again I slid my Bible down to my knees, but this time not with cynicism. It was to allow the truth of the psalm to seep from my mind into my heart.

I had been reaching out for God, rather than to Him. It is easier to look *for* God; but to do so is to disregard ways in which He has already made Himself known to us. If we look *to* the God we know – however dimly that may be – we allow our vision of Him to be enlarged. If we cannot or dare not come any closer than to touch the hem of His garment then that gesture alone brings us towards an encounter with Him which engages our whole being.

And I had been reaching out empty-handedly, waving my arms like a drowning person out of my depth awaiting rescue. Desperate as I was, I did not really want to do more than simply stick my hands up out of the water and let God pluck me out. In my emptiness I saw no way other than to wait. I fancied receiving a dose of God's kindness and power. In fact probably I was seeking not so much to touch God, as to touch healing.

Thus I had not really liked to read of the psalmist doing more than merely wait. I had not wanted to see that his hands had not been empty like mine. While he had waited for God, he had held on to something which I did not want to hold on to: his trust, his faith, and his acknowledgment of his enemies. His prayer was thus not so much a demand of God as it was offering God whatever he could, and letting God do with it what He willed.

There is a sense in which we need to allow for hope. It is not sufficient to expect it to come to us. To be downhearted was reasonable: more reasonable than to hope. And reason won over faith, until my prayers stopped centring on my problem and began to focus on God Himself. When we are faced by hard times, we need not look only at the trauma. We can actually give our energy to make space for hope – make space for God – by seeking Him.

There's a score across the sky, there
Where an aeroplane's just been
Cutting it and marring it
Slicing it in two

There's a score across my abdomen
Where surgeons' knives have been
Cutting me and marring me
Slicing me in two

There's a score across my life, Lord
Where deepest hurts have been
I am so marred
and cut apart
in many, many ways

The trail above me's fading now
Blown across the sky
The scar across my abdomen
is fading with the years
But the scar across my life, Lord,
Never can be swept away

Save me from seeing only hurt;
Show me Your hand as well:
For with one touch

You leave Your mark
Changing me,
not marring me
Leading me
to You.

Hating pain as if it were my enemy was fruitless, disheartening and introspective. What God wanted was for me to see that it was the destructive inner attitudes such as self-pity which were my real enemies.

The darkness of a womb

Last year, just after I had finished updating *A Pathway through Pain*, and before it was even published, the dark cloud of illness returned to me again. I had written with great glee that I had now improved, rejoicing that three years had elapsed since my last operation. For two years I had not needed to be admitted to hospital and as time had passed I had grown stronger and my hopes rose higher and higher that I was now better: better meaning well, not just temporarily improved. Then, unbidden, the old and familiar pain crept back. For a few weeks I fought on until, one afternoon in early January, I could no longer overcome it with a sensible lifestyle and positive self-talk. With numb horror I heard the words from our doctor which I had come to hope I would never need to hear again: that I had to go to hospital.

Not again! That was my inner cry. But the trouble was, it *was* happening, yet again. That is my story; just like another person's story of a nagging spouse. It is the 'yet again' which causes as much pain as the irritation itself. For me the hospital bed, with its metal bars, represented the prison in which I was caged against my will. Where is freedom in darkness? Where was this hearty hope for 'light at the end of the tunnel'? Was there ever going to be an end to my tunnel?

While pain screamed and the peritonitis ran its ugly course, with all the distressing symptoms of an internal abscess, I could not consider the questions. I simply endured, choiceless. I cannot even say that I did anything as positive as grit my teeth. Only, time passed.

Then suddenly, one morning in late February, I woke to the familiar sounds of the ward but I knew that something was different. It was still night time but, when I opened my eyes, it was as if a star had appeared in the night sky. There was light. What was it? How did it come? I cannot tie it down like that. But there was a sense of promise. There was courage, waiting for me to take hold of. There was a knowledge: a deep, unshakable certainty in the truth. To describe this as trust would make it sound like the fruit of my own effort, which it was not. The light in the darkness convinced me that I could trust God. I knew it as definitely as one knows from an invisible, intangible scent in the air that there is perfume. That morning, the air was redolent with the fragrance of God Himself.

With a taste of freedom which had been so utterly absent, I knew that God had created darkness. I found myself recalling that each day of His creation had begun, not with dawn, but with darkness. 'There was evening, and there was morning, one day.' To wait for dawn and believe that that was the beginning of hope was to overlook the creative value God placed on the night time itself. This was not the dawn. It was the light shining in the darkness.

Another thought came to me, too, that morning. I knew that a womb – that place of immense creativity – is a place of darkness. Darkness is the perfect environment for new life to be conceived. And therefore, I pursued with rising excitement, our darkness could be the perfect environment for nurturing new life. Of course, like mothers in early pregnancy, we may be so distracted by feeling sick and weary and uncomfortable, we may not even know that there is any new life growing. Nevertheless, I felt sure that much of our darkness is a womb.

We might cope with traumas by jollying ourselves along, endeavouring to look on the bright side and ignore how grim darkness can be. Some Christians tell themselves, or others, to ignore whatever hurts and simply keep looking to Jesus. When they quote Bible verses to substantiate such exhortations they may sound very spiritual. But while such coping mechanisms may help, they are not the whole story. If, in fact, the darkness is an important place, we need to be careful not to deny the very place where new life – yet unseen – is being conceived, and fed, and nurtured.

While we are waiting for dawn to break, or for new life to peep out from its hidden place, we stumble around in the dark. Often we feel we have nothing to offer to God: nothing except a blind and weary blankness. However I am beginning to believe that God wants us to offer even that. For then we know that whatever comes to us is not because we have reached for God, but because He has reached out to us.

8

Being touched by God in the depths

The sky was deep black
yet at the same time bright with sunlight
— astronaut, Aleksei Leonov

After we have offered our tears to God – our tears, our emptiness, our feeling that nothing is worthwhile – when there is nothing more we can offer to Him, then we know how utterly dependent we are on His reaching out to us and touching us.

At a wedding in Cana, in Galilee, Jesus changed water into wine. As then, so now He changes the water of our tears into something rich and valued. In His own time, He gives us the nod, telling us to draw on the water which we have shed, and taste, and see for ourselves what He has done. We cannot engineer such a transformation for ourselves; we are entirely at God's mercy.

The transformation which Jesus brought about in Cana was immediate. First fill the jars, He said, then draw on them. For us it may be weeks or months between filling our jars (or our handkerchiefs) and drawing from those tears. It may even be years before

His healing touch becomes evident to us. Or we may never see it for ourselves.

In 1989, Matthew and I both went through a time which stands out in our minds, not only as one of the hardest times, but also as a time when we embarked on an extraordinary experience of having water changed into wine. We did not know then that that was happening; I seem to recall that there were many days when we felt as if God were doing nothing at all. Certainly we both felt impotent and unable to change our situation; something which I found particularly hard as it went against the very grain of my personality. Matthew, watching, was more aware of an anger with God – this God of power and miracles Who was not using His might to change events. It looked like a story where God was doing nothing, changing nothing.

This was the summer of 1989 when I had entered another severe phase of illness and I became acutely ill once more. The consultant who was looking after me was a skilled and gentlemanly surgeon, and immediately after examining me he called Matthew in to his room. It was plain from his whole demeanour that he was bearing bad news. He explained with a sense of some urgency that a full-blown infection had returned: once again I had acute peritonitis. He had found my blood pressure low, my pulse rate high. I was weak and gravely ill. His voice, always calm, spoke with particular tenderness. He told us that although normally he would have operated on the suspected abscess before it burst, he feared I might not survive another operation.

The treatment he chose was less traumatic, more conservative than surgery, consisting of drips and

injections while my condition was monitored inten-
sively. During the following few days my life simply
ebbed away. Friends who came to visit me, who had
previously been astonished at the fighting spirit they
had seen helping me through bad times before, now
saw me and were shocked. This was the most traumatic time of all for Matthew. He could see a special
peace settle over me, increasingly, as my hold on to
life weakened. He was the one left struggling, fighting back the tears, needing the grace to let go of me
but not feeling that grace to be evident as he wanted.

I recall one particular night when Matthew and
I had said goodbye to one another. We were serene
rather than sombre; we were both held in an embrace
of God's peace. I watched Matthew leave and saw his
closeness to tears as he struggled to release his hold
on my mortal life. And as I prayed for him through
the following long hours, the picture which came
to me was of Jesus transforming water into wine.
Weakly grasping a pencil, little by little as I lay that
night, I wrote to Matthew:

> Do not weep
> when my body will rest at last
>
> Do not weep
> when its loud demands
> are silenced at last
>
> Do not weep
> when writhing can cease
> and I can lie quietly
> beside still waters
>
> Or if you do;
>   if tears well up
>   in the chalice of your soul

Give God your tears

And let Him change them
into rich wine
consecrated to Him

We knew, both Matthew and myself, that we
could give God absolutely nothing except miser-
able, watery wretchedness. And as I lay through
the small hours of that night, aware of the burden
of my every breath, I found the beauty of hope.
This can have been little less than the touch of
God. Quite unbidden I knew that God could take
our supposed nothingness and replace it with the
richness of Himself. I knew, too, that He could take
what is transparent – feelings – and suffuse them
with what has substance – faith. Just like water
into wine.

In the days and nights which followed I poured
out my soul before God, writing many more psalms.
What brought me a quiet sense of awe was that it
was as if God were pouring out His soul before me.
That hospital bed in Fazakerley hospital became
holy ground. The overwhelming hallmark of all
that I wrote is not my weakness but God's healing
presence.

There was no miracle which one could point to,
and quantify, to use as 'proof' of God's work.
Physically I did not find 'rest at last', either in
death or in cure. My body's loud demands were
not silenced and, however much my soul had
been stilled, my body's writhing did not cease.
Gradually, however, I began to improve until I
was out of danger, if not out of pain. Under the

care of that tender and competent consultant, the infection cleared and I became better enough to be discharged from the ward, at least for a while before the next and terrible onslaught.

God's transformation in Matthew was different and not even apparent for a long time. Looking back, I would say that it took six years, until the beginning of 1995, before we saw anything of how God had ministered to him in those depths. Then, it was as if many parts of the scene were re-enacted with the same, dreadful demand that Matthew should sit again by the side of my hospital bed and see life drain away from me. But this time Matthew was not the same. This time he did not restrain his tears: he wept beside me. He wept not so much for this episode on its own, but for the previous time, and the times before that, when he had been too busy being angry that God had not made me better. Then there had been no space for weeping. This time, he was given the courage to let go of himself and let himself taste the saltiness of tears.

One day he was 'caught' by our family doctor who, after visiting me in hospital, called at home straight away to see how Matthew was coping. In her presence, too, he wept. Matthew, the man before a woman. Matthew, the priest before a lay person. And although she sought to console him, she also talked of his tears as a gift. It was with regret that she reflected on those husbands who could not – would not – weep. She said they were the poorer because they did not have the resources which Matthew had, to weep over their wives' appalling illnesses or invasive disabilities.

Weeping as a resource? Yes. When offered to God, our tears release us to abandon ourselves to

Him without restraint. Even physically the way in which our tears spill over and tumble down our cheeks gives a picture of how, once we finally allow the barriers of restraint between us and God to be broken down, then there is a great spilling out of lots which formerly we had kept safely in check.

It would be easy to write as if suddenly God made everything seem bearable, or happy; or to sound as if His miracle were complete. But God's miracles are not always as clear cut as that. Just as wine is comprised mostly of water, but with special other ingredients which make it so intoxicatingly delicious, so with God's transformation. Mingled with our tears and hurt and grief, we discover the wonder of the presence of God and His mystery. In the darkness there is light. I cannot quantify this, nor identify God's arrival, any more than one can specify what time dew falls. Only, we know when it has fallen because our feet become wet from walking on the grass.

I can only say simply that God has left His mark. We know He is God. We know He is able to do (in St Paul's words) 'far more abundantly than ever we ask or even imagine' and that, if and when He does not do what we ask, He is doing something more important. I do not understand fully, and often I do not like it, but I know that the God of miracles is always at His transforming work within and around us, whether we recognise His hand or not.

Surprised by God

As I write I am just back home after leading a week-end conference. One of the most potent sessions was also the most painful. Several people were touched by God in their depths and the surprise was that what they received was not at all what they had expected (or asked for!). People changed from looking for the miracle they wanted (that God should lift them out of their terrible circumstances). They were surprised by God Himself.

The turning point for one man was being asked quite simply, 'What one thing hurts you most?' He had been horrified at the question. He had so many hurts; he had so much to say – had always said, when asked what hurt him. Now he had been asked to write down the one thing which hurt him most.

The hurdle was huge and the man had to take time to think. Was it his physical pain, which dominated his every move? If he put that, he would be omitting to write of the different hurt of his wife not understanding. Or his friends . . .

At this point the man realised that the greatest hurt he carried around with him was not physical but something else: something he had never acknowledged before, either to others or to himself. Plucking up his courage, and trusting that no-one would read over his shoulder, he wrote down his one thing that was probably hurting him most.

At this stage, I had asked everyone in the group to write a letter to God: their own version of Job, chapter 3. This fantastically graphic chapter contains Job's heartfelt 'splurge' of feelings, including the utter despair he felt at the dreadful depths to which God had let him sink.

The man thought, 'I can't do THAT!' But, faced by the choice between fifteen minutes of twiddling his pen or fifteen minutes which could, possibly, help (already he noticed that those who had begun looked deeply involved, as if this exercise were helping them; though how, he knew not!) he mustered a final scrap of courage and began, very tentatively, to write his first words.

Within a few phrases, he found he could not stop. Words flowed from him, and with them came emotions he had never known he had. Tears began to slip down his cheeks, but now he was not even considering what anyone else might think of him. He was stating his case in a letter to God. He was there, in it, before the throne of God. And God was listening.

After he had finished the man recalls little else of the evening except that he felt at peace. That night he slept well. If he had needed a sign that something had happened in him, that was it. He knew he had received no less than the grace of God Himself.

Another lady was somewhat upset at first during one session; a lady who had been comfortable with her faith, and comforted by it. During the quietness of a meditation I had asked people to picture God as Father. She was afraid. But something drew her on and she stopped looking to her own fear. As she imagined herself coming nearer to her heavenly Father, she tried to picture Him.

In her mind's eye, she saw that her Father's eyes were not lustful and frightening, but were filled with compassion. His arms were held open to her in welcome and not – as she acknowledged for the first time – to grab hold of her menacingly. She had always known in her mind that God was trustworthy but, that day, her knowledge began to trickle into her feelings. Like a toddler she dared to take her first rather clumsy steps towards His embrace. As she did so she pictured God coming to gather her into

His arms like a shepherd tenderly lifting a lamb. She could almost see Him reach down and pick her up with a tenderness she had never before experienced from her own father. She knew, now, that she was safe. She began to relax, allowing Him to cradle her in His arms. His hold was secure. She knew, too, that here she was close to His heart.

On the following morning this lady, normally shy, leapt to her feet to tell everyone at the conference of her miracle. If she had needed a sign that something had changed, that was it. She had found courage. 'This is a whole new beginning!' she beamed. 'I can come to the right place, now, for my security. I can draw close to God's heart without being afraid.'

This lady had never before realised that she had had any hesitation in coming to God as her Father. She had never even realised that she had blanked off all the images of her earthly father's touch. She had not known there was an aching void within her, waiting to be filled with the tenderness of God. For fifty years she had prayed for God to come near to her and meet her in her loneliness but suddenly, that weekend, He surprised her. He touched her in her depths which were deeper than she had ever acknowledged. His drawing near to her had begun with discomfort: a discomfort which she had tried to bypass for half a century. Always before she had trusted God to lift her over the terrible hurdle she did not want to face. Instead, He had taken her through it, by a most unexpected route; but He had made her feel deeply cleansed and free.

One of our hopes when we reach out to touch God is that, since He is light, our darkness will be turned to light and all will be well. That is the truth, but I am convinced that it is not the whole of the truth. We also need to discover that God is in the darkness. There is nowhere where we can go where we are away from Him. He is everywhere, as Psalm 139 makes so clear. He is not to be found more fully in miracles or in healing, or in any signs and wonders. He is found in the dawn of light, of course; but He is also waiting to be found in the darkness where we fear to look.

The silence of God

We may long to hear God's voice and be disappointed if all we hear is silence. We do not know how to receive His silence. We take that to be the absence of His voice. If we are anything like the psalmist, or Job, we rail at Him with our cries: 'Where are You, Lord? How long will You stand so far off?' We are slow to grasp what He offers in the 'still, small voice'. I once read that a more faithful translation of this 'still small voice' of God that Elijah heard (1 Kings 19:12) is 'the sound of gentle silence'.

This gives me hope. It offers the possibility of my learning to hear His voice, not always as words, but in the silence I loathe. It gives me hope that the sound of gentle silence will turn my turmoil into stillness. It begs for me to tune in to His way – His gentle, silent way – instead of continuing to rant and rave at Him for not speaking. And in the silence, then I sense the rippling echo of Jesus's words when He calmed the storm: 'Peace, be still'.

At other times, after I have prayed for God's blessing, I still feel empty and blank. Other people have described this experience as their prayers hitting the ceiling; I would say it is worse than that.

At least if they had hit the ceiling, the plaster would look battered and bashed! Whereas the worst aspect of praying and still feeling empty is that God seems to be unmoved. It seems *nothing* has happened. We are left feeling horribly hollow.

I am moved every time I read the story of Hezekiah whose illness brought him close to death. He felt absolutely crushed by God. 'In the prime of my life must I go through the gates of death and be robbed of the rest of my years?' (Isaiah 38:10). He felt that God had been brutal with him, and he told Him so. 'Day and night you made an end of me,' he said. God had let things go too far without coming to the rescue. Hezekiah's house had been pulled down; Hezekiah had 'waited patiently' but, instead of receiving help, he said, 'like a lion he broke all my bones; . . . I cried like a swift or thrush, I moaned like a mourning dove. My eyes grew weak as I looked to the heavens . . .'

Yet, despite God having allowed things to get worse, the miracle was that Hezekiah ended up being grateful. 'Surely it was for my benefit that I suffered such anguish.'

How could he have been grateful? How can such suffering as this be good? Hezekiah did not justify it. He simply said that his suffering had helped him to know God's greatness and holiness. It had caused him to learn the place of humility before God Himself. 'What can I say?' he asked himself aloud. 'He [God] has spoken to me, and He Himself has done this. I will walk humbly all my years because of this anguish of my soul' (Isaiah 38:15).

Whenever I wish to give vent to my frustration and disillusionment, that sentence stops me in my tracks. The place of humility before God is not a place to which, naturally, I aspire. I am ambitious and competitive, and I get a thrill from achieving things which I call worthwhile in this life. I thank God that He is turning my ambitions upside down. I thank Him that He has let me hear the call to humility before Him. And I do not write that lightly. I know that His means of giving me even a tiny idea of my place before Him, has been through anguish of my soul.

Once during a period when I felt bleak and empty, I spent about twenty-four hours at a convent, specifically in order to pray. I longed for God to draw near to me and touch me. At the beginning of my time I wrote in my prayer diary, 'Lord, please lighten my darkness. Fill my emptiness.' However, it was only during my time of being steeped in an atmosphere of prayer that I began to realise the foolishness of my thinking. Here I was yet again, wanting to feel better for praying.

As I read my written prayer, it was as if God asked me, 'How much would you want to pray if you did not feel any the better for it? Would you still pray then? For *My* sake?'

So much of my life has been geared around myself. Self-expression, self-fulfilment, self-actualisation. I have been bringing my self-orientation to God and asking Him to bless me. In prayer I have been touched by God's holiness. I cannot prove that. I can merely see the sign that, after that twenty-four hours at the convent I knew my attitude had been changed. I wanted to pray, 'Lord, please empty my fullness.'

Whenever we are touched by God in our depths we discover a little more of Who He is, and how much we mean to Him. He reminds us that He truly is the Sovereign, and not we ourselves. Then we find that our prayer is changed, from us bossing Him around to us enquiring what He wants. Then, and only then, can we abandon ourselves into His hands, no matter what we are to go through. Then we can begin to follow Him, which was the first thing Jesus asked His disciples to do; something we try to avoid whenever we pray, turning the words of His command around until we feel in charge and we ask God to follow us. However, when we are touched by Him we are humbled; we see our folly and He stirs our desire to follow Him.

When we are touched by God we stop praying like little Sunday School children, asking God to listen to our catalogue of troubles. We allow ourselves to be taught by Him, just as the boy Samuel was taught by Eli in the temple. Then we can begin our prayer with, 'Speak, Lord, for Your servant is listening,' instead of insisting, 'Listen, Lord, for Your servant is speaking.'

When we are touched by God we come to know our need of Him all the more. That is a place which is pitied by the world, including other Christians who, like Job's comforters, decide to pray for us. They remain perplexed if our need is not satisfied. However, in God's eyes, we are not to be pitied for knowing our need of God. Jesus said that that is a blessed place to be.

Some Christians believe very firmly that God touches us because we ask Him to. Mostly, I prefer to leave such discussion to the theologians. However, although I admire those people, I have wondered how we can dare to imagine that God only blesses us when we ask Him to. I recall when I was at my worst physically, when every breath

I breathed was a noticeable effort. Even the tiny movement of flaring my nostrils enough to let the air pass seemed to demand something from me. Each time I wondered whether I would 'make it' the next time. What I recall is being convinced, then, that every breath we breathe is because of God's gift. And we are not even aware of the gift of our breath until it is almost taken away. In how many other ways is He blessing us and giving us life? How can we say God only blesses us when we ask Him?

God has more riches than ever we recognise. He gives us more than we ever ask, or even imagine. Perhaps we need to be more prepared to let go of our long-held faith and hold, instead, to God Himself. In our deepest suffering He becomes more important than any hopes we may have had for His blessings. In our deepest suffering, He becomes more important than our faith.

9

Touch . . . Do not cling

Many Christians are 'Christaholics'
and not disciples.
Disciples are cross-bearers . . .
– writer Calvin Miller

When we have reached out from our depths and
touched God – and, even better, been touched by
Him – we naturally want to hold on to Him and
hold on to whatever He has given us.

When we lived in Runcorn I used to look out of
my study window to an area of woodland beyond
our garden fence. I used to watch the scene change
through every season. One autumn, one tree caught
my attention. It seemed to be reluctant to shed the
last of its leaves. Long after all the other trees were
stripped bare for the winter, this tree clung on to its
last leaves. They were so distinct I counted them:
there were twelve. It was as if the tree did not want
to let go of what had once been so beautiful. A few
weeks earlier those leaves had displayed a glorious
array of rich autumnal colour. In the summer they
had been a lush green, representing the fullness of

summer growth. Earlier still, in the spring, they had been tiny buds which had brought excitement and anticipation of new life.

But as I watched from my window I was struck by how ridiculous that tree looked. Winter was beginning; this was not the time for the beauty of spring, or summer, or autumn! Was the tree ashamed to be seen in its bareness? Was it trying to protect itself from the stark reality of natural life, as if being clothed in last season's blessings would protect it?

And it seemed to be a parable about my own life. I, too, can be so thrilled by growth within me, or God's rich blessings, or by the beauty which He bestows, that I can want to cling on to those blessings beyond their season. I can even use holy language to make my folly sound acceptable. Yet it is not always appropriate! Holy-sounding words can hide the fact that I am ashamed to be seen bare, without any blessings. The psalm which I wrote that winter bears witness to that discovery.

Wind-blown, leaf-swept
bare trees.
But see!
Not all are bare.
Not that tree.
Twelve leaves are still there . . .

Branches holding
Fingers stretching
As with desperate resolve
to cling on . . .

Cling on to what has been:
Cling on to new Spring birth-that-was
Cling on to lush Summer growth-that-was

Cling on to rich Autumn beauty-that-was
It's the last dregs now . . .

It's
just a tree.
Always there
hiding beneath
Now exposed:
Now
Just a tree
with twelve leaves

Lord,
Give me new birth
  But not to cling on to;
May I always be renewed

Give me lush growth
  But not to cling on to;
May I always be growing

Give me rich beauty
  But not to cling on to;
May I always be Yours

Let me cling only
to being
bare before You.

God gives us blessings appropriate to the moment;
different according to the season. His blessings are
for us to touch, and be touched by, but not for us
to cling on to.

Often we reach out to touch God in one place and
are touched by Him elsewhere. For years Matthew
and I asked Him for healing, and what we received
was a glimpse of the greatness of God. When God
is not obedient to us, and does not do what we ask

Him to, we usually feel disappointed in Him. Many people become disillusioned in Him. Being touched by Him, however, is more than having God do what we ask. God is bigger than that.

Last week I telephoned friends whose daughter has just had a malignant brain tumour removed; now she is undergoing chemotherapy. They asked all their friends to pray for her red blood count to be raised. It had measured only seven that day, instead of the normal twelve to fourteen, and she was to have a blood transfusion the following day. 'Please pray!' they urged.

Several people prayed in faith. At a meeting in their home everyone wanted to pray, together. It was as if God were urging each person to pray. They were of one mind. It felt a special time and they were all filled with a particular strength and a hope which seemed to be from God Himself.

The following day, when the girl went to hospital to be cross-matched ready for her transfusion, the level of red blood cells had increased. Remarkably, it had gone from seven to eleven. The hospital staff, surprised, took another blood sample to check the result, not once but twice: the instant readings of this test are not terribly accurate. Each time the result came back the same: the red blood cell count was eleven. There was no need for a transfusion. That little girl and her parents returned home from hospital elated, and they shared their joy with those who had prayed.

'God has answered our prayers!' they exclaimed. 'Be encouraged: and we must keep praying.'

But this week, God is not answering like that. Friends have kept praying as requested, but God has not done what so many people have asked Him to do. This week it is the white cell count which is low – well, zero. In their darkness, the girl's parents are holding fast to their faith and are again urging us friends to 'pray harder' for her white cell count.

By now I want to put up my hand and say, 'Hang on a moment!' We do not pray in order to twist the arm of a reluctant God. We do not need to make sacrifices, as to pagan gods, and 'pray harder' to persuade Him to be kind, or good, and do what we say. I see God's hand in leading people to prayer and I rejoice with my friends in every sign of light in their long dark tunnel. But I would be uncomfortable if anyone were to suggest that prayer ensures that we are given a cocoon of protection against all human tragedy. I would be uncomfortable if we can only say that God is good when He does what we ask Him to; when He does what we endorse.

Are we so absorbed in our own immediate needs that we do not dare to believe God may be good even when we cannot see His goodness?

While Job went through the mill, his friends told him he could alter the course of his suffering if he did this, or that. However, that was not what God said! He said that some suffering has '*no point*' on earth (Job 2:3).

The problem for Job was that God did not reassure him of this truth. We only know that God had said this in heaven, not on earth. Indeed, it was the fact that God hung back in the situation that Job found so difficult. When eventually – eventually! after Job had despaired of hearing God again – God spoke, He told Job's comforters that they had been wrong. They had been wrong to talk of God as they had (42:7), suggesting that Job's continued suffering had anything whatsoever to do with Job not praying aright. In His speech, which takes up the final four chapters of the book of Job, God made it very clear that He does some things which we know nothing about. We want to have Him tied up and neatly boxed; God says we cannot. We cannot understand all that He is doing.

Jesus told His followers that some suffering (He was talking about a blind man) had 'nothing to do with his sins or his parents' (John 9:3 GNB). We humans – and especially the Christians, I think! – seem to be much quicker to apportion blame, suggesting that people who suffer have not prayed the 'right' way, compounding the misery of the one who is suffering.

There is an allusion to this truth in Ephesians 3:10 too. Paul says that God uses the church 'in order that . . . the angelic rulers and powers in the heavenly world might learn of his wisdom in all its different forms' (GNB).

God is at work, and not only on earth but on a wider canvas than we can ever imagine. He does not only have the whole world in His hands, but all of the heavenly realm, too. According to that verse in Ephesians, God sometimes uses us to prove a point in the heavenly realm – whatever this means! – and I only understand it in the light of that verse I quoted above from Job 2:3. We know nothing of God's meetings with angels when they come to present themselves before Him (Job 1:6 and 2:1). But while He says there may be 'no point' in our suffering on earth, there *is* a purpose in the heavenly realm.

Too often we attempt to restrict God to the God whom we know. He is more than that; always He is more than we could ask or even imagine. However much He has already blessed us, He is able to do more. However much He has hung back from us – or seemed to – He is more than we have so far glimpsed. We only see in a dimly-lit mirror now, but in fact He is much brighter and greater than our dull image of Him reflects. We may always hope in Him: we will never be disappointed in Him. Any disappointment we have is in the images of Him which are less than He is.

Too often we attempt to confine God to the God whom we know, who has bowled us over by some amazing miracle or blessing. At a simple level, we go through periods when we feel the better for our prayer time, pepped up by God, and given fresh purpose to life. But we insult Him if we imagine that that is all God is: One who makes us feel better and who gives us a sense of purpose. To love and worship Him for that would be mere cupboard love! He offers us more than that, much more; and He wants more from us than our weary souls waiting to be refreshed by Him.

I caught myself treating God as if he were a panacea one morning when I was in the middle of writing. I stopped work and sat down comfortably for a break. I had a cup of coffee which I hoped would perk me up a little, and I also had a couple of painkillers as my abdomen was aching. I also (rather virtuously, I confess!) had my Bible and by the end of my break I felt a little better for turning my thoughts Godwards.

I was just dragging myself up from the comfort of my beanbag when I suddenly realised what I had been doing. I had been trying to make myself feel good. The caffeine and the painkillers were resources to help me. And I was treating God no differently. I hoped that a 'dose' of Him would give

me a spiritual and emotional buzz to help me with
what I was doing.

I sat down and wrote a type of confession:

Too often
I treat You
as a coffee-break God

Giving You a slot
in my day
From which I leave
refreshed
but ready to return
to 'the rest of life'

Yet You, Lord,
are a living fountain
welling up constantly
bubbling perpetually

Never to be confined
to one cup, like a dose,
to be drunk
and then emptied
Once each day
(or twice
or maybe three times!)
ticked off, and signed:
Drug administered

No, Lord!
May I drink from You always.
For the more I sup
Then the more I thirst
for 'the rest of my life'
to be irrigated
by channels which overflow

> from a constant exchange
> at Your wellspring.

Too often we reach out to touch God, and we do not give enough time to be touched by Him. Or we are so busy telling Him what we need, we do not give our attention to where He is.

At a church near to us in London a teenager was, one day, healed of deafness in one ear. I was not present when it happened but I caught the absolute thrill of one of my friends who had been there and those who heard about it afterwards.

The girl was fourteen years old. She had lost her hearing on one side after a severe ear infection twelve months earlier. She had had hearing tests and had been told that her ear had been damaged irreparably. Her parents, unsatisfied with the lack of treatment at the first hospital, took her to a chain of consultants, but eventually they resigned themselves to what both consultant and registrars said to them. Their daughter was deaf in one ear. They were told that a hearing aid would not help because of the damage at the back of her ear.

Then at their church one Sunday the congregation were given an opportunity to be prayed for individually. This girl went forward. And during the prayer time she felt a searing pain and then she heard her father whisper. 'Can you hear me?' came his gentle voice. And with a shout of utter elation she cried, 'Yes!'

Everyone was ecstatic, from the girl herself to her family and the whole church as they realised what the shouting was about. When she went to the hospital later that month, the results of her aural tests were plotted, as always, on a graph. The comparison with the previous tests was completely different. This time they showed that her hearing was normal in both ears. The surgeon, a Hindu, commented rather mysteriously that 'these things do happen now and again'. He also asked if their God was an ear, nose and throat specialist.

That family had reached out to touch God and they were touched by Him in a remarkable way with a remarkable cure. Their response was to give praise to God, accepting the girl's healing as a gift unearned, but given from His store of goodness.

The problem came when others, both inside and outside their church, talked as if a repeat performance of this gift could be anticipated. There was a subtle implication that God will always do this type of miracle for whoever asks. I found this very difficult. I am sure that God can always do this. However, I also know that He does not.

To be touched by the miracle of God is infinitely reassuring; to cling to His miracles is eternally tempting. But many people are profoundly hurt by Christians who say, in effect, 'Look what God has done for me; He will do the same for you too if only you would ask in the right way.' We do not know that He will; only that He can. We do not know if He will work a miracle for us again; only that He can. We cannot pin Him down. God once said, 'No-one can put a bridle on a crocodile and make him do what he's told; how on earth do you think you can tame ME or pin ME down, when I made the crocodile in the first place?!' (Job 41: 9–10, my paraphrase).

When we have been touched by God we can believe, 'This is *it*! Now I have experienced the fullness of God; I have been made whole by His resurrection power.' If ever we believe we have had all we need from God, we are deluding ourselves. We cannot contain God; there is always more of Him than we know or experience. However delicious a taste we have had of His goodness, it is only a foretaste. He always has more in store for us.

After His resurrection Jesus gave two apparently contradictory instructions to two people. To one He said, 'Reach out and touch me'; to another He said, 'Do not cling to me'. I do not think these are opposites. There is a time for each one. We need to hear both. To carry out each of Jesus's instructions is hard in its own way; each demands our courage.

When we have recognised Him as having done great miracles we need to hear Him say, 'Do not cling to me'. It was to Mary Magdalene that He said this when she had seen Him for the first time, risen from the grave. She ran towards Him but Jesus told her to restrain herself. 'Do not hold on to Me,' He said, telling her instead to move on from that place, and go and tell others about Him. The power of His resurrection was not to be confined to one place. She had not seen everything yet. Jesus did not want Mary to confine Him in her experience.

Isn't it puzzling that Jesus should ask us to restrain ourselves from holding on to His miracles? Is He telling us not to reach out to Him at all when we are distressed? I think not. Later in the same chapter (John 20) Jesus invited Thomas to 'Reach out your hand and put it into My side. Stop doubting and believe.' When we doubt, we need to hear His invitation to touch Him. To respond with faith at such a time is difficult enough. It is easier for us to listen to our doubts, our questionings, our cynical 'Yes, buts', or our 'But what ifs', or our indulgent cry, 'I need Him to do everything for me; I can't reach out to Him!'

When we touch God, yet without clinging to Him, prayer begins to be transformed. We discover that we can begin to let go of demanding what we want; then empty words become rich communion. When we let go of our hopes that God will repeat yesterday's miracle we can receive, instead, something fresh. And what He chooses to give us at different times will change, according to His agenda, His goodness.

The prophet Jeremiah spoke of God's goodness to people who could not see it for themselves. He told them God's message: '"for I know the plans I have for you," declares the Lord, "plans to prosper you and not to harm you, plans to give you hope and a future. Then you will call upon me and come and pray to me, and I will listen to you"' (Jeremiah 29: 11–12). This is God's promise. We do not always feel it to be true, but we are invited to trust Him in our darkness.

Another prophet declared God's goodness to be much greater than we can see. Habakkuk was certain that no catastrophe, however terrible, could make Him doubt that God is in control. He said, 'Though the fig-tree does *not* bud and there are *no* grapes on the vines, though the olive crop fails and the fields produce *no* food, though there are *no* sheep in the pen and *no* cattle in the stalls, yet I will rejoice in the Lord, I will be joyful in God my Saviour' (Habakkuk 3: 17–18, all italics mine).

Why? How? we ask. Because Habakkuk trusted God to be Sovereign, as he said in the next verse. 'The Sovereign Lord is my strength; he makes my feet like the feet of a deer, he enables me to go on the heights.'

God is not confined to working miracles which change events and which we recognise. His miracles also enable us to get through the rocky pathway ahead, to stumble blindly on through amazingly grim times.

It is very tempting, when we have been touched by God in the depths, to want to hold on to Him. But while our holding can be very good, it can also become the kind of clinginess associated with a child who does not want to grow up. Dependence on God is good, but a refusal to live in partnership with Him, or a refusal to share His yoke, is to disregard a different aspect of His invitation.

God is Sovereign, which means that He is not only Lord in our good moments: our moments when we see Him, moments which are like successes. He is also Lord in our failures.

Lord in our failures

Some years ago at the prize-giving ceremony during an annual conference for Christian booksellers, one lady who was presented with an award stood before hundreds of people. She glowed with pleasure and reward from all her hard work. She leaned towards the microphone and breathed with a huge smile, 'God is good!'

I remember the intensity of my discomfort. While I could see she was thrilled, I could hear her using words to define God according to her feelings. I wanted to leap up and shout out, 'But God is good whether you won a prize or not! There are hundreds of people here who haven't won. God is still good and they want to trust Him.'

I suspect the strength of my reaction came from the

fact that I was very ill at that time. Attending that one session alone was taking more from me than I had to give. Matthew had brought me to be interviewed about my newly-published autobiography but I was very weak. Even though I had a couch to lie down discreetly at the back of the hall, I could feel energy drain from me as I sat waiting for my turn to go up on the platform. It was as if life itself were draining from me.

I knew that I wanted to tell those people that I had written that book specifically to emphasise the truth which is often hidden. God is good even when life is bad. I wanted to encourage the booksellers not only to sell stories of miracles where everyone lives happily ever after (if they do!). I wanted to say that God's unseen goodness is around us when we cannot see it: when we feel dreadful, when it is an effort to push one foot after another to move forward at all; when we fear we may not make it to our goals. When we cannot see God's goodness we can doubt that it exists. But it does. He promises us that. When we cannot feel God Himself, He is still there. Indeed He is so close He is not there, but here.

I have never forgotten the strength of my reaction to that prize-winner. I have seen it re-emerge in parallel, but different, circumstances. Last year I read a heart-warming testimony in a magazine which reflected the writer's conviction that God is good 'because' his prayer had been answered. He had prayed for a new chapel since his was cramped and smelly and nasty; and soon afterwards his prayer (and his request to those in authority over him) had been granted.

'Alleluia!' he wrote in his article. 'God is faithful.'

Once again, beside my pleasure for him I also prickled with discomfort. What if his group had *not* been offered a new chapel? Would that have meant that God had not been faithful? Because in fact there are Christians in many places all over the world who only have pokey, noisy, stinking places which they honour with the name 'Chapel'. God is still faithful even though they have not been given luxury lounges! In fact, one is moved to read of their trust in Him despite their poverty. Such people make God the focus of their worship: God Himself, and not His blessings.

There is a lovely song about God's blessings which includes the lines,

Let the weak say I am strong
Let the poor say I am rich
Because of what the Lord has done for me.

I also love to sing that song reversing those words,

Let the strong say I am weak
Let the rich say I am poor
Because of what the Lord has done for me.

When God hits our strength and makes us weak we are hurt and angry and mystified and many other reactions. But eventually, as we are ready to take His hand and accept His touch, we discover the blessedness of being stripped bare before Him. Vulnerable, weak, poor and afraid, we come to Him. And while others might pity us, or tell us they will pray for us, I know that God our Father accepts us. His eyes crinkle with the lines of deep, unfathomable, patient love which melts our shame and draws us closer. He smiles upon us with the delight of one who has always longed to share the warmth of His affection. He stretches out His arms with the kind of invitation which welcomes us before we have even arrived. And He reaches down to us, just as we are, gently lifting us until He holds us close to His heart. There we find ourselves nestling, enfolded in His gentle might, listening to His pulse, feeling His breath fall upon our forehead, hearing His whisper. In His hold we are made ready to touch the depths with Him.

10

Touching the depths with God

There is silence and darkness and airlessness.
We cannot reach out to touch and reassure.
This is the ultimate emptiness.

              – Brian Keenan

Brian Keenan was taken hostage in Lebanon in 1985. For four and a half years he was held in inhuman conditions, tortured sometimes physically, but mostly mentally and emotionally. In *An Evil Cradling* he articulates a depth of pain into which few of us enter but with which, strangely, many of us can identify. He wrote about the 'ultimate emptiness' of his time of solitude in a darkened cell, 'There is silence and darkness and airlessness. We cannot reach out to touch and reassure.'

There is a devastating, appalling emptiness of not being reassured when we have been badly wounded. Pain can be so destructive, and such a waste, it is only when we touch the depths with God that we glimpse any meaning to it at all. Then the focus shifts from ourselves and our suffering, to Jesus and His sufferings.

Corrie ten Boom was the first person of whom I read who did this. Imprisoned by the Nazis in the notorious Ravensbrück camp, she was stripped naked along with the hundreds of others, to be leered at and jeered at by the cold-blooded guards. While all her fellow women prisoners stood shivering in silent horror at their corporate humiliation, Corrie's faith told her more than that Christ shared in her suffering. She heard an invitation to have her eyes opened to glimpse, and then share, in Christ's suffering.

'Betsie!' she whispered to her sister standing to attention ahead of her in the line. They were not even allowed to wrap their arms around themselves to create the tiniest comfort of warmth or modesty. 'They took Jesus's clothes, too.'

Her sister bit her lip as she pictured Him being stripped naked in front of mocking people, just as she was at that moment. 'And I've never even thanked Him!'

I have not had to go through any suffering like a Ravensbrook camp. But having read of Corrie and Betsie ten Boom there, I see that every little suffering has the same invitation for us to glimpse what Jesus went through, and thereby to share with Him in His depths.

It is easy to say, 'But God had not been through what I have been through.' I remember myself feeling terribly alone because Jesus did not have a prolonged illness. 'His suffering ended,' I wailed inwardly. 'The pain He had to endure on the cross was awful, yes, but at least by dusk it had finished. That's very different from pain which goes on for years, with no prospect of an ending. And anyway, His suffering had a purpose: He was saving the whole world! Mine isn't worth while like His: if only it were, it would not be half so bad. He cannot truly understand what endless, pointless suffering is like.'

How little I truly understood! For God does endure an ongoing pain which I can only ever glimpse: the pain of loving with an unrequited love. We exacerbate His pain whenever we misunderstand His love, or misconstrue it, or pontificate with our sweeping accusations which reveal more of our ignorance than His truth.

'God cannot understand about the suffering involved in caring for a handicapped child!' some may exclaim. 'He is in His heaven while I, alone, have to get up through the night and demonstrate patience through gritted teeth while my child screams in apparent agony when I caress him, or who spits out the drink I have lovingly prepared for him . . .'

Oh, but God knows; indeed He knows more about having handicapped or disobedient children than ever we can fathom. For He is our Father and we, His children, often reject the food and drink He proffers to us. We often react with violence when He reaches out to caress us. He Who is Love always acts with patience, even when provoked by our repeatedly wayward behaviour.

'Jesus never married; He could not know what it's like to live with a spouse who does not love! He could not know what divorce, or separation, is like!'

How ignorantly we speak of Him! For He does indeed know what it's like to live through separation. He has declared His love for the Church, saying we are His bride, and He has promised to love us eternally. And how do we love Him in return? So poorly; so feebly; so unequally compared with His sacrificial love poured unrestrainedly out for us.

Not only so, but also God wants us to see how He

grieves for us. I have come to believe that He wants to share His pain with us, not in order to make us feel guilty but in order that we may know the love which motivates Him.

One of the prophets in Old Testament times, Hosea, was asked to prophesy not only with words, but also by giving his whole life as a parable of how God feels about His people. God asked Hosea to marry a woman who was to become a prostitute. God wanted to communicate that what Hosea endured gave a picture of what He was enduring. Hosea had a terrible lot to put up with. His wife went out flaunting herself in the streets before other men, believing Hosea didn't love her enough. When Hosea gave her gifts, she did not thank him – did not even recognise that the gifts were from him. She showed to her lovers a gratitude which should have been directed to him, gaining sympathy by telling them that Hosea didn't care. This, said God, was what we do to Him. We flaunt ourselves before other gods to worship (money, power, ambition), believing His love falls short of our needs. When He gives us gifts, we do not thank Him, nor even recognise that they are from Him: we accept them as if we had earned them from elsewhere. And all the time God waits faithfully like a husband awaiting His true love, just as Hosea was asked to demonstrate with his wife.

God does not only understand our suffering, whatever it is. He does not only share with us in our pain. He also invites us to see how our pain can be a window to let us see the pain which He endures for our sakes. Whatever our pain, it is only a dim reflection of His. I am convinced that there is always the possibility for us to look less to ourselves and our pain, and more to Him.

It took for me to be hurt quite often, psychologically, before I even began to emerge from feeling my
own hurt into realising that my experience was also
an invitation to glimpse how I – we – treat God and
thereby hurt Him.

It happened when I felt very alone in the everyday
slog of pushing through life. Others had shown their
care for my ongoing illness but life goes on and they
had their lives to lead apart from visiting me for
months on end. Prolonged suffering is more tedious
than acute: in its lack of drama it can be more
lonesome. Nobody could rescue me from the fact
that my life involved a great deal of physical pain.
It was my responsibility to move from resignation to
acceptance and, frankly, I didn't want to make that
jump. I was stuck at feeling resigned to it. I suspect I
was afraid of accepting it since that step would have
been so healthy psychologically, I probably feared
that I would no longer be eligible for more sympathy.
And I felt quite justified in wanting more!

One day the doctor called and decided that he
needed to increase the amount of pain relief I was
taking. He prescribed pills for me to take later, but
administered the first injection himself. When he had
done so he wiped the needle site with an antiseptic
swab so there was no trace of bloody trauma, and
washed his hands. As he turned from the basin he
summarised his decision calmly, 'You've drugs for
the pain and drugs for the nausea: just shout if you
need more.'

Something in his manner epitomised an attitude
which caused me to feel terribly alone. He seemed
unwilling to acknowledge the depths of my emotional state which accompanied so much physical
pain. As I watched him dry his hands I felt a

sudden, unexpected rush of lonely anger. It was all right for him, I thought: he could wipe away every visible trace of having come close to my agony. He could drive off and remain distanced without ever entering into what hurt. He could wash his hands of me emotionally and keep me at arm's length. It was as if he had convinced himself that there was no more to pain than administering pain-killing, awareness-dulling drugs.

At one level, of course, he was right. Doctors are trained to diagnose and treat physical signs and symptoms of illness. If they did not distance themselves, they would lose their objectivity so essential to wise decisions. Yet at another level, his emotional withdrawal caused me to feel treated without being comforted. There is an old maxim written above the entrance to the Mayo Pain Clinic which reads, 'To cure sometimes, to relieve often, to care always'. He seemed to have forgotten that.

Left, as I was, emotionally on my own, I had only God to turn to.

So I prayed. As I did so, I made my hand available for Him to hold. I did not torment myself by telling myself it was pathetic to use God as a prop whenever I feel lonely. I *did* feel lonely and I *did* want God to take my hand and comfort me! And suddenly I knew that His hand, too, had been made available for me to hold. He had had to bear this kind of aloneness, too, in Gethsemane. And I knew, with a tremble of privilege, that instead of my waiting for Him to take my hand, I could take His. I could touch His depths; just a little anyway. That was a pivotal moment. My thoughts were switched from my aloneness to His. I thought of Gethsemane, trying (clumsily, no doubt) to put myself in His sandals as I imagined Him on that night. There had been no 'treatment' to help Him; there had been no escape from what He had had to face. All He had asked of those with Him was that, while He bore His anguish, they should stay awake and watch with Him, and pray with Him, and demonstrate that they were alongside Him.

Jesus's friends could not do that. Despite His begging them to stay awake, they fell asleep. Although they saw with their physical eyes how much He was suffering, so they could later recall His agony and describe how perspiration had poured from Him like great drops of blood; yet with their inner eyes they could not see how He had needed them. Jesus was alone.

On the day of that doctor's rather harsh-sounding words I dared to stop waiting for God to reach out to me, and I pictured Him waiting for me to reach out my hand to His. As I did so my loneliness stopped being the hateful wall which had surrounded me and it became instead a window. It became a means of my beginning to see God's point of view. But what I saw was not an ancient tableau; it was a beginning of a whole new perspective of prayer.

'You've drugs for the pain
And drugs for the nausea:
Just shout if you need more.'

More?
More than that needle and syringe
with tiny impregnated antiseptic
to wipe away the trace where it went in?
More than little white pills
proffered on clean hands?
They are my treatment.

'Is that all right?'
'Yes, all right.'

A smile exchanged
     though not with my eyes.
A wave goodbye
A car driving away.

There is no more.
And a tear falls quietly
Quickly rubbed away.

Lord, guard me from self-pity:
You, too, were not comforted.
Your friends slept
unaware of Your inward struggles
while you sweated out Your anguish.

Engender in me a sensitivity
towards others
which I long for them to show
towards me

Engender in me a sensitivity
towards You:
Because I only ever glimpse Your struggles

Pain – and I mean any kind of pain – can be an opportunity to feel with God, and picture Him; or it can be an opportunity for us to stay curled up around our own hurts and keep concentrating on ourselves.

I am reminded of the six-year-old boy, whom I mentioned in chapter 3, whose dying was so memorable for all the staff in the ward in Edinburgh. When he took his mother's hand, he was comforting her rather than vice versa. He was not responsible for his mother, but he was made to love and love gives. He touched her in her broken-heartedness. In a similar, though not parallel, way I believe we who are made to love can touch the hem of God who is broken-hearted over us. We cannot change Him; we cannot seek to console Him; but I believe we can share in His suffering in a mysterious, unquantifiable way.

While driving down a dual carriageway some time ago, I once drew alongside another car in the middle of the rush hour traffic. A woman was driving; I guessed she was the mother of the three children all in the back. She was clearly very fraught, and with much reason: the baby was crying and the two older children were fighting with one another across his baby-seat. Poor soul, I thought. For once I did not have my two young children with me but that was a rare treat, then, and I could well identify with her irritation. As the traffic slowed to a standstill and we sat side by side in the queue, I expected her to turn and shout at them all to be quiet. I wanted to catch her eye and give her a smile to communicate that I was a fellow mother and I understood. I, too, had been in her position. But the moment she faced my direction and knew she had been seen, she quickly turned away. She would not let me give her the smile I felt for her.

I found that moment so frustrating! It was understanding I had wanted to show her, and acceptance, and a caring kind of companionship. But she was so afraid of the condemnation she must have been dreading, I had no chance to convey to her my own thoughts.

My smile, unreceived, rejected, hung frozen on my lips. Then suddenly I saw a parallel. 'Is this how You feel, Lord?' I prayed immediately. 'Wanting to convey care, and understanding, and acceptance; waiting for us to look to You so You can share Your love with us, but we will not allow You to do so because we're so busy dreading Your condemnation?'

Once again there was an invitation to share the depths with God.

Another day I struggled to church feeling pretty ill and, after the service, I was asked how I was. The question was asked mechanically but I answered more truthfully than routinely, having been reprimanded often for not saying when I am unwell. Each time I did so, I felt rebuffed. At this point I should acknowledge that probably I have done exactly the same to other people: instead of listening to what they are telling me, I have heard their point of view and given them mine, almost making conversation into a competition to see whose remarks are the more interesting. Why do I do it? Listening is a skill to be learned.

I returned from church after the service mindful of how much God, too, has to endure our being poor listeners. We ask Him questions, yet we will not wait in silence for Him to speak. Thus I wrote:

'How are you?'
    The question is asked:
    I'll put out feelers
    tentatively.
    If they care
    they'll release me to say more.

'It's not been a good week.'
'Oh dear, I'm glad you're better now though.
I'm glad to see you:
I wanted to talk . . .'

Better?
Who said I feel better?
Because I've put on a dress
dragged myself out
and smiled?
Say no more, Jane.
Just listen.

'How are you?'
'I've been a bit sore actually.'
'Poor you. Yes, I've had a sore foot:
broke it years ago.
I'll tell you about it . . .'
Say no more, Jane.
Just listen.

Is this what you do, Lord?
Just listen?
No chance to speak
for our moaning
and droning
about ourselves
our trivia
repetitively.

Lord, teach me to pray:
to stop informing You
of history You already know.

When I ask you to speak
May Your word not simply remind me of myself

May I listen wholly
And feel with You
And think with You
And picture You
in all I hear You say.

Pain empties us. It empties us of physical strength; it empties us of answers; it empties us of self-esteem. After we have been emptied our prayers, if we are honest, include a shout to God, 'Can't you see? This pain is thwarting my plans; preventing me from succeeding in my career; emptying my life of what I find fulfilling . . .'

God does see. Jesus emptied Himself of all the fullness of heaven. God came to our world, not to sweep away all evil with a magic wand to wave to the accompaniment of triumphant fanfares. God lay in a manger, utterly vulnerable, small and apparently useless. If ever we feel emptied, then we can begin to touch the depths with Him. We touch the hem of the garment of humility which He wore when He came to this earth.

Mirroring God

I visit, quite regularly, a convent where – usually – I find prayer much easier than at home, enhanced as it is by the atmosphere of many nuns' prayers. During one of my retreats, unusually, I spent the whole of my time there feeling unmoved by God. I did not feel the better for being steeped for twenty-four hours in that atmosphere of prayer. I did not feel strangely warmed by His presence. I did not feel the clouds of tedium lift between me and Him. My spiritual journey was still duty: I had been given no buzz of feeling especially blessed.

Just before departing, I went for the last time to the little chapel and, alone, I knelt on the floor at the back. Ahead of me, suspended from the ceiling, was a life-size cross painted with a picture of Jesus. I gazed at that painted figure with the kind face. I longed to see His face come to life. And I cried out, 'Come to me!'

Nothing moved. The candle by the altar burned unflickeringly. The darkness hugged the nuns' stalls. Nothing changed in response to my prayer.

I had had such a disappointing day, I was already tempted to think that the lack of movement in response to my prayer was inevitable. However, into the silence as I knelt on that cold hard floor, a tiny thought struggled to the surface of my mind. We are made in the image of God. Was my heart's cry a reflection of His? Had he initiated the cry in the first place, and I merely echoed Him?

'Come to Me!' It was as if Christ Himself were looking down to me, uttering the very words with the same longing as I had reflected back to Him.

I was hushed, for a while, until the truculent side of me bubbled up to the surface again. But I *had* come to Him! Wasn't it a bit unfair if Jesus was beseeching me to come to Him? He was the one who was transcendent. I wanted to put the ball back into His court. I altered my prayer.

'I need You!' I begged Him.

Again, through the silence, came the realisation. Again I heard my words as a mirror of His.

I need you!

Could it, I wondered, have been God's voice that I was echoing? Does He yearn for us with those same words?

Of course, not all my prayers reflect Him. Some arise from selfishness. Yet some do indeed reflect His heart's desire and after spending a full day feeling spiritually dry, I came away with a richness I had not dared to hope for.

St Paul wrote to the church in Philippi, 'I want to

know Christ and the power of his resurrection *and* the fellowship of sharing in His sufferings' (Philippians 3:10, italics mine). Sharing Jesus's suffering is very different from sharing our own. Often, we can aim to transfer the weight of our own yoke on to others. To partake in the fellowship of Jesus's suffering is to take our part in sharing the weight of His yoke. It means – at least in part – taking each moment of our own pain as an opportunity to enter into the awful light that He has suffered likewise. The power of the resurrection is much more appealing than the fellowship of His sufferings; it is more popular, more attractive in its optimism. But to talk of that alone is to share only a part of the story.

This is one of the treasures of darkness: that in our depths, in our darkness, we stumble upon the awe-filling truth. We are invited to share with Christ in His agony.

> When pain was great
> I gave
> whispering,
> 'For You, Lord, I'll do this!'
>
> They did not know
> the cost to me
>
> They saw no pain
> so they could not recognise
> my sacrifice
>
> And they accused,
> 'You did not give enough!'
>
> So now I want
> to resent
> to be angry

to shout, like a child,
'They're not fair!'

I want
to laugh at Your command
that we should give
and never count the cost

Yet, You give
when we do not know
nor appreciate
the cost to You

You give
when we do not see
nor recognise
Your sacrifice

You give
though Your pain is great
whispering,
'For you, whom I love, I'll do this!'

11

Treasures of darkness

If you want to see wonder
you need only look at the night sky
– astronomer during a radio discussion

John was a composed, well-educated man who had
had a very successful career. He had earned himself
such a reputation at work that, for several years after
he retired, he used to be invited back to his work
as a consultant to advise on specific projects. John
apparently coped remarkably well with life's grim
times. He invariably appeared cheerfully optimistic,
refusing to be dragged down. When problems on his
committee could not be bypassed, he would remind
his colleagues that 'every cloud has a silver lining'.

Those who knew John outside his work were
divided in their comments. He had a sick wife
and one adult daughter who was depressed to the
point of feeling suicidal. His brother, living nearby
in the large family home, was bitter about his plight:
his marriage had failed and he had been left alone
with a violent, handicapped daughter. Some friends
looked at John and admired him all the more for

his ruthless optimism despite such hurdles. Others grieved for him because they felt he was unaware of how his very refusal to look at pain was causing hurt to those who were in the cloud.

John, they said, had to live on the crest of the wave. It was like an addiction for him. He did not want to contemplate the fact that, whenever a wave has a crest, it also has a down-pulling current. A wave is formed out of tension and contradiction.

One evening, not long before he died, John was watching television. Between programmes there was an advertisement for one of the BBC's special features about the Second World War, celebrating the fifty-year anniversary of its end. John never watched war programmes ('Depressing stuff! Just remember that we won!'), but the tiny snippet in the trailer that evening was sufficient to throw a switch in his mind. He saw the battlefield where he had fought; saw, for a second or maybe two, the place in which he had survived but his friends had died. He saw that he had only survived because he had caused others to die.

Suddenly he could not be proud of his bravery and courage which had earned him several medals, proudly kept behind glass on display in his lounge. Suddenly he saw that, by purring with pride at his own achievements, he was denying the horror of what he had done. His ambitions fulfilled had had a cost. He had killed and maimed; he had looked down the barrel of his gun and hated. Worse than that, he had done so with boyish glee, enjoying himself, refusing to contemplate the suffering which rippled on in the wake of his success. And after the war, his ambitions at his work had similarly demanded a cost of others.

This moment of revelation was as agonising as it was unwelcome. John did not know what to do with the thoughts which now hurled themselves at him like bullets. The advertisement was over and a new, comedy programme beginning. He poured generous drinks for his wife and himself, and tried to drown himself in the empty laughter on his screen.

But the following morning the torment had grown worse. It was as if John had watched his own life acted out on a stage, and he saw it through a different pair of eyes. His so-called bravery now seemed like cowardice, for he had never before had the courage to look at the pain of life. But the images in his mind were too vivid for him to bypass them any longer.

John could not telephone his friends because, he reasoned, he could not shatter the admiration and respect which he had worked all his life to gain. Must keep a grip on things! So he telephoned his local priest, asking him to call and 'chat something over'. Within an hour the priest was in his home listening to some horrifying aspects of John's life which poured from him like pus flowing from an abscess lanced. John wept tears of remorse for what he had done and for how he had denied it to himself. He wept over his pleasure in his fulfilments which disregarded the cost. The priest asked him if he wanted to change and, when he nodded, pronounced an absolution.

The priest then gave John a penance, according to the Catholic tradition, which on this occasion was to read my book of psalms. (Yes, I do see the funny side of that!) 'If you want to stop denying the dark side of your life,' said the priest, 'read this.' Which is why John wrote to me – we had not seen one another for some considerable time.

'Jane,' he began. He told me his story. 'I have

not read your books before, not liking the idea of anyone bellyaching about their suffering. I write to say I'm sorry, and thank you: both.

'I had not considered before that ignoring wherever there is hurt is denying life. But since pain is a fact of life then, by denying it, I suppose I have been denying a part of life. I feel now I must face all of life and not just a part of it. It all feels jolly alien and bloody hard.

'I'm sorry that, until this penance, I had not considered the riches you have obviously found. However, now I must thank you and most especially for one phrase in *Faith in Flames* which reads, "Free to be fragmented, I am loosed . . ."

'I feel I have been loosed from a lifetime of denial and I must thank God.'

John died very shortly after this. His death saddened me enormously, for it seemed too soon. He had not had time to live out the consequences of his new-found freedom. I often wonder to myself what effect it might have had on his daughter if he could have begun to acknowledge the dark side of her cloud and not insisted on talking of the silver lining. If he, as a father, had entered into the cloud: is that not what means most to a child (however old), that a father should put aside his grandeur and be beside them at their level, in their broken humanity? Or if he had visited his embittered brother and sat on the floor with his niece 'wasting' time playing childish games. Would that not have been like visiting them in their prison, imparting his resources as father and brother by his very presence? I wished he could have lived out the new way of living he had perceived in his penance:

Pain's constrictions
  contradict smugness
  confining
  coercing

Like a drawstring
  gathering in the fullness of my life
  restricting
  restraining
  tightening limitations around me

Unable to escape
I am able only to accept

And I am loosed

For when I am broken
So too are those boundaries
Which make me look whole

Free to be fragmented
I am drawn to my Father
Whose one caress
Gathers me gently
with whispered promise
to make me whole
His way

Pain as healing?

I am beginning to think that an important part of healing is the capacity to be broken and to share that brokenness with God, reflecting Him. This was the treasure for John: to dare to acknowledge the darkness and discover freedom within what had looked like an inescapable prison.

Some years ago I was to give a talk at a festival

celebrating the ministry of the Retreat House in Chester diocese. During the week beforehand one of the Sisters telephoned me to check that all was well. She asked how I was and, sensing that she was enquiring genuinely rather than making ritual conversation, I told her.

'I'm floundering around here,' I told her. 'I feel exhausted, drained and confused. It's terrible! I've no idea how I can prepare my talk when I'm feeling like this.'

I expected the Sister to reply with an encouraging kind of remark. I knew that some people, recognising how I felt, might have been sympathetic; others, I imagined, would no doubt have told me that the Devil was getting at me.

The Sister's response was shockingly different. 'Oh,' and her voice had a definite quiver of excitement. 'God *is* at work in you, isn't He?!'

Through clenched teeth I thanked her and asked if she could explain what on earth she meant.

'Well, He's got you where you have to rely on Him. I'm so glad. I *am* looking forward to the Festival!'

That Sister saw what I could not: the treasure in the darkness. She recognised the holy ground of suffering. Her thinking appears to be upside down. Yet it is only when we step out of the conventional world view that we can recognise any such blessing at all.

This does not mean (at least, not to me) that all is well that ends well. When C. S. Lewis was at the end of his emotional tether after the death of his wife, his colleagues – men at the pinnacle of academic excellence as Oxford dons – felt impotent, knowing they were unable to relieve the acuteness of Lewis's grief. One man dared to ask him one day, 'Is there anything we can do?'

Lewis's reply was curt. 'Just don't say it's all for the best, that's all.'

Similarly for Sarah, whose story I recounted in chapter 3, the treasure for her was not that after the darkness had passed she would know it had been worthwhile. She was not left with something better after her baby had died. She was left with emptiness. She was worse off than before. Only a callous, unfeeling person would urge her to praise God for her baby's death.

No. Sarah had to stay with the loss. The darkness remained. But in staying there, *there* was Truth, too. All the evidence shouted that God could not be good. The truth was that God does not impose dreadful things on us, disregarding the cost. Sarah knew that the only peaceful course was to trust in God's goodness; that He was trustworthy. The truth was stronger than the lie.

In watching Sarah and many others – including, even, looking back on my own experience – I do believe that the insight into God's truth is not necessarily permanent. About ten years have passed since Sarah's baby died and, when I quoted the words she had written to me, she looked astonished. 'Was that really what I wrote?' she asked. She reread her diary and was moved to read the evidence of God Himself enabling her faith. Grace had been given to Sarah; grace which is God's gift, His treasure. We can pick up our convictions and put them down several times in the course of our pilgrimage.

Some pain feels 'worth it', like the soreness of an eye operation which restores sight. Those moments of pain are usually soon forgotten because they dissolve with the stitches. That is very different from pain which continues to make its impact on one's very soul. Then we may see a good purpose to it but, equally, we may not. When we do not, then we are stripped of all our neatly packaged philosophical answers and we stand naked before God feeling vulnerable and humiliated. In God's hands, however, humiliation is transformed into humility. There have been times when I have witnessed such a transformation and I have had to ask whether pain itself might be a part of our healing.

I do not write that lightly. I could sound so callous if I did not also write with tears of helplessness and sorrow over many people's stories of anguish and suffering beyond human endurance. However I cannot write of death without also writing of resurrection. Perhaps this has been brought home to me very clearly through the writings of a man whose promising life was thwarted – or apparently so – by the poor health of his wife and the repeated trauma they had to endure through five miscarriages. One of his poems speaks eloquently of his life while it was being shattered.

there are cracks in my world
i noticed them one day
and now they are everywhere
sinister hairline cracks that start
and finish out of sight
cracks that grow and gape
and laugh at my certainties
my world has been declared unsafe

i have tried to paper them over

paint them out
shift the furniture to hide them
– but they always return—
cracks that hang like question marks in my mind

but

they have thrown it open to new horizons
drawn back curtains
raised long-closed shutters
one day i looked and
a crack had become a window
step through, it said, what have you to fear?
do you wish to stay in your crumbling room?

and then i remembered a childhood dream
watching the egg of some exotic bird
oval and perfect, spotted blue and cream
(i wished to hold that egg and keep it on a shelf)

but

as i watched it, cracks appeared
tiny fissures spread like zigzag ripples
it broke in two and life struggled to its feet
wet and weak and blinking-at-the-world

without those cracks that egg could hold
no more than rotting stagnant death

without its cracks my world would be
a room without a view
cracks may be uncomfortable disturbing gaps

but

could it be i need them?

do you believe in cracks?

because i keep searching for God in the room

and find He is hiding in the cracks
Dave Bookless, 1990

The treasure in this man's darkness is something which, often, we do not even notice in our busyness with this world. He told me once that what he most looks for and values is when people's faces come alive with recognition at what is important in life. His face, too, came alive as we questioned together whether pain can be part of healing.

I have no doubt that pain is a thief, a robber. I have watched it cling like a leech to people – patients I have nursed, friends, spouses of colleagues – and it has sucked their very lifeblood until they have been dead, yet left carrying the intolerable burden of their body. I have listened to men weep great sobs as they have talked of pain stealing away the laughter from their marriage – and not just the laughter. It is the very soul of a person that pain grips; it lynches the personality, draining away hope until all one is left with is the wretchedness of a body too exhausted to love.

Pain is a thief and a robber, stealing souls from bodies and minds.

Pain is also a gift. It transports people from remote independence to vulnerable dependence. It transforms from hard know-alls to stumbling questors. Therefore we hate it: we have to learn how to do otherwise. It leads us into awareness of our need for God. When it persists or burns more fiercely it makes us shout in prayer at the God Who seems not to have heard us. He *can't* have heard if He isn't *do*ing something! And as our shouts grow louder and the pain remains we are forced to listen to our prayers.

To hear our prayers is a gift which silences our loud self-orientation and opens the door to let us hear how our Saviour is praying.

If pain goes on yet more; if it goes on beyond what we feel we can bear, we have no option other than to look at the darkness and face what is happening to us and in us. That is when we enter the process of healing. For healing is not an event, but a process. And pain can be the vehicle, not the enemy.

A few weeks ago I caught a snippet of conversation between a group of scientists on the radio, about space and the planets. An astronomer – I did not catch his name – made a little aside as he talked of his work. 'If you want to see wonder,' he said, and his voice was filled with awe, 'you need only look at the night sky.'

Immediately, I thought of our desire to see God's wonder in our metaphorical 'night sky'. I thought how easily we assume that, since God is Light, we will see His wonder in the brilliance of those miracles which shine out like stars. However I am convinced that that is only a part of the truth. If we want to see wonder, we need to look at – not away from – our night sky.

The treasures of darkness do not shine so brightly that all darkness is dispelled. They are treasures of darkness. They are God's promise.